Richard L. Nash

30 Days to Better English

by NORMAN LEWIS

SCHOLASTIC BOOK SERVICES
NEW YORK · TORONTO · LONDON · AUCKLAND · SYDNEY · TOKYO

This book is sold subject to the condition that it shall not be resold, lent, or otherwise circulated in any binding or cover other than that in which it is published—unless prior written permission has been obtained from the publisher—and without a similar condition, including this condition, being imposed on the subsequent purchaser.

Copyright © 1954, 1956, 1957, 1958, 1961 by Birk & Co., Inc.
Copyright © 1964 by Scholastic Magazines, Inc. This edition is published by Scholastic Book Services, a division of Scholastic Magazines, Inc., by arrangement with the author and Birk & Co., Inc.

7th printing .... February 1974

Printed in the US.A.

TO
Mary, Margie, and Debbie

Contents

PART I: Test Your English

FIRST DAY: Test Your Pronunciation 2
Three short but revealing pronunciation tests give you an accurate indication of how you sound to other people.

SECOND DAY: Test Your Vocabulary 4
React to thirty specially selected words to discover whether your vocabulary is average, good, or superior.

THIRD DAY: Test Your Spelling 7
In a few moments you can find out whether your spelling is as good as it should be, or whether you make errors you're not even aware of.

FOURTH DAY: Test Your Grammar 10
Do you generally use words correctly? Are you usually sure, or only half sure? Let's put it to a test.

FIFTH DAY: Just for Fun 13

PART II: Say It Right

SIXTH DAY: Practice in Pronunciation 19
Can you pass this easy pronunciation test?

SEVENTH DAY: More Practice in Good Pronunciation .. 22
> Here are twenty-five important words that poor speakers say in a slovenly fashion. How about you?

EIGHTH DAY: Still More Words That Fool the Unwary 27
> Examine four final categories of English words; then check the success of your learning in Part II by taking a pronunciation test that most unsophisticated speakers would do very poorly on.

NINTH DAY: Just for Fun 31

PART III: Improve Your Vocabulary

TENTH DAY: A Simple Program for Vocabulary Improvement 36
> To increase your vocabulary at a prodigious rate, you must learn to be on the alert for new words.

ELEVENTH DAY: Is Your Vocabulary Average, Good, Excellent, or Superior? 46
> Four more tests to tell you where you stand.

TWELFTH DAY: A New Way to Build Your Vocabulary 48
> Roots provide clues that can help you decipher new words for yourself and increase your vocabulary.

THIRTEENTH DAY: Let's Learn Ten New Words 62
> A quick warmup that will help you add some short and expressive terms to your vocabulary.

FOURTEENTH DAY: A Challenge to Your Vocabulary 65
> Here are fifty more words that should be in every educated person's vocabulary. How successfully can you *learn them?*

FIFTEENTH DAY: Just for Fun 70

PART IV: Spell It Right

SIXTEENTH DAY: Special Tricks That Will Make You a Better Speller 74
> *Learning to be a good speller may seem difficult, but there are tested short cuts to quick and permanent mastery of the words most people misspell.*

SEVENTEENTH DAY: More Memory Tricks to Make You a Perfect Speller 82
> *By now you should be convinced that mnemonics make mastery of correct spelling practically effortless. Today you conquer once and for all time twenty-three new words that are frequently misspelled.*

EIGHTEENTH DAY: And Still More Tricks 86
> *Another fifteen words you can conquer through mnemonics.*

NINETEENTH DAY: Some More Spelling Tests to Keep You Alert 92
> *By now you should really feel your spelling ability improving—but don't relax. The next five tests will check on your learning and introduce some new demons for you to conquer.*

TWENTIETH DAY: A Final Acid Test of Your Newly Acquired Spelling Skill 96
> *When you've mastered all of the hundred words tested in this chapter, it will be a cold day in August before anyone can ever stump you again!*

TWENTY-FIRST DAY: Just for Fun 100

PART V: Speak Correctly

TWENTY-SECOND DAY: An English Test for You 106
> *Let's find out if your everyday English is as good as you are.*

Twenty-third Day: The Most Confusing Verbs in the English Language and How to Get Them Straight 113
No other verbs cause as much trouble as lay *and* lie. *Now you can begin mastering them by learning a few simple and easy-to-apply principles.*

Twenty-fourth Day: Final Steps for Mastering *lay* and *lie* 116
Today you nail down your understanding of these troublesome verbs and prove to yourself that you can now avoid all confusion.

Twenty-fifth Day: How to Find Your Way Through Singulars and Plurals 120
Do you have to stop sometimes and wonder whether to use is *or* are, has *or* have, was *or* were? *Let's discover how easy it is to decide, once you're sure of the rules.*

Twenty-sixth Day: Just for Fun 126

PART VI: The Final Days

Twenty-seventh Day: How Would You Solve These Five Grammar Problems? 130
Like *or* as? Me *or* I? None are *or* none is? Between *or* among? Sure *or* surely? *How do you usually say it, and are you right or wrong?*

Twenty-eighth Day: Seven New Problems to Pit Your Wits Against 134
Is a singular or plural verb used after who? *What is the difference between* childlike *and* childish? *When do you feel* bad, *when* badly? *Which is correct,* we boys *or* us boys? *More excursions into the kind of pesky little problems that make English so difficult.*

TWENTY-NINTH DAY: Eight Final Problems and How to Tackle Them 137
> *When are we* disinterested, *when* uninterested? *Is* phenomenon *singular or plural? How about* measles, mathematics? *Is it all right to use* due to *as a conjunction? Are* try and come *and* older than me *correct English? Some more notes on present-day standards of educated Americans.*

THIRTIETH DAY: Just for Fun 142

ix

OTHER BOOKS BY NORMAN LEWIS

Dictionary of Modern Pronunciation
How to Get More Out of Your Reading
New Guides to Word Power
Power with Words
The Comprehensive Word Guide
The Lewis English Refresher and Vocabulary
   Builder
The Rapid Vocabulary Builder
Thirty Days to a More Powerful Vocabulary
   (with Wilfred Funk)
*Twenty Days to Better Spelling

*Available in an SBS edition.

PART I

Test Your English

>Do you make embarrassing errors in pronunciation, spelling, grammar, word usage?
>Is your vocabulary fresh and growing, or do you use the same old tired words over and over?
>In short, does your English work for you or against you? Here's your chance to find out!

The words you use can work either *for* or *against* you, and in a real sense, *you* are the one who makes the choice.

For, rightly or wrongly, you are often judged not only by what you say but, more immediately, by how you say it. Your language, whether in speech or writing, announces to the world: "This is the kind of person I am."

The relations you have with other people are largely dependent on words. You communicate to others your feelings, your needs, your ideas, your reactions in words. More important, you continuously present yourself in words.

Just what kind of person do others see when you speak, when you write a letter, when you turn in a composition, enter an essay in a contest, draw up a club report? Part I will help you discover what your spelling, pronunciation, and grammar say about you.

FIRST DAY

Test Your Pronunciation

Three short but revealing pronunciation tests give you an accurate indication of how you sound to other people.

Does Your Pronunciation Help You Put Your Best Foot Forward?

In the following three tests, check in each instance the pronunciation you naturally and habitually use. Do not be influenced by what you think may or may not be "correct."

> The symbol ə indicates the very slight vowel sound heard in the first syllable of **commit** (kə-MIT') or the last syllable of **Linda** (LIN'-də).

Test 1: Do you avoid common but glaring errors?

If so, you will check the preferable pronunciation of at least four of the following five words:

1. **Italian:** (a) ə-TAL'yən; (b) eye-TAL'-yən
2. **genuine:** (a) JEN'-yoo-in; (b) JEN'-yoo-wine
3. **theater:** (a) thee-AY'-tər; (b) THEE'-ə-tər
4. **nuclear:** (a) NOO'-klee-ər; (b) NOO'-kyə-lər
5. **pronunciation:** (a) pro-NOUN'-see-ay-shən; (b) pro-NUN'-see-ay-shən

Check your results: 1-a, 2-a, 3-b, 4-a, 5-b.

Test 2: Does your pronunciation meet "educated standards"?

If so, you will check the preferred pronunciation of at least four of the following:

1. **percolator:** (a) PUR'-kyoo-lay-tər; (b) PUR'-kə-lay-tər
2. **preferable:** (a) PREF'-ər-əbəl; (b) prə-FUR'-ə-bəl
3. **phraseology:** (a) fray-zee-OL'-ə-jee; (b) fray-ZOL'-ə-jee
4. **extraordinary:** (a) EX'-trə-OR'-də-ner-ee; (b) ex-TRAWR'-də-ner-ee
5. **naïveté:** (a) NAY'-və-tee; (b) nah-eev-TAY'

Check your results: 1-b, 2-a, 3-a, 4-b, 5-b.

Test 3: If you use an uncommon word, do you say it correctly?

If so, you will know the correct pronunciation of at least four of the following:

1. **epitome:** (a) EP'-ə-tome; (b) e-PIT'-ə-mee
2. **awry:** (a) ə-RYE'; (b) AW'-ree
3. **machinations:** (a) match-ə-NAY'-shənz; (b) mak-ə-NAY'-shənz
4. **inexorable:** (a) in-EX'-ər-ə-bəl; (b) IN'-eg-ZAWR'-ə-bəl
5. **ribald:** (a) RYE'-bawld; (b) RIB'-əld

Check your results: 1-b, 2-a, 3-b, 4-a, 5-b.

SECOND DAY

Test Your Vocabulary

React to thirty specially selected words to discover whether your vocabulary is average, good, or superior.

Does Your Vocabulary Reflect Your Mental Stature?

It was discovered, some years ago, that one particular ability was common to all successful business executives. At the Human Engineering Laboratory, then affiliated with the Stevens Institute of Technology in New Jersey, aptitude tests were administered to thousands of adults from every walk of life. Without exception, the top-scoring names showed the greatest skill in just one field: vocabulary. And, again without exception, everyone who had an extensive vocabulary also held a high position in his chosen field.

Surprisingly, formal education turned out to have less relation to the vocabulary score than might reasonably be expected. One man—a major executive of the telephone company—made a better showing than any college professor who took the tests, yet he had left school at fourteen!

The three tests that follow will show you whether your vocabulary is average, good, or superior.

Test 4: Do you have an average vocabulary?

If so, you will have no difficulty matching the following words and meanings. Seventy-five per cent of the people tested knew the meaning of all these words.

1. imminent   (a) cleanse
2. fluster   (b) flashy
3. rigid   (c) confuse
4. purge   (d) bring back to former excellence
5. rehabilitate   (e) hinder
6. latent   (f) pretend
7. gaudy   (g) stiff
8. feign   (h) coax
9. cajole   (i) hidden
10. impede   (j) likely to happen in the near future

Check your results: 1-j, 2-c, 3-g, 4-a, 5-d, 6-i, 7-b, 8-f, 9-h, 10-e.

Test 5: Do you have a good vocabulary?

Decide whether the following words and meanings are *similar* (S) or *opposite* (O) and indicate in the space provided. Only 49 per cent of the people tested knew these words. You have a good vocabulary if you get at least eight right.

1. **myriad**: small in number _____
2. **panacea**: cure-all _____
3. **opulent**: poverty-stricken _____
4. **eschew**: avoid _____
5. **nefarious**: wicked _____
6. **incarcerate**: imprison _____
7. **ameliorate**: make worse _____
8. **candor**: hypocrisy _____
9. **taciturn**: talkative _____
10. **verbose**: wordy _____

Check your results: 1-O, 2-S, 3-O, 4-S, 5-S, 6-S, 7-O, 8-O, 9-O, 10-S.

Test 6: Do you have a superior vocabulary?

Determine which of the following statements are *true* (T), which *false* (F), and check in the space provided. Only 22 per cent of the people tested knew the words in boldface type, so yours is a superior vocabulary if you can react correctly to eight or more:

1. **Obsequiousness** is a sign of pride. _____
2. **Parsimonious** people are extravagant. _____
3. Peace in the world is an **exigency** of the moment. _____
4. The wolf is a **predatory** animal. _____
5. An **aquiline** nose is straight. _____
6. Vice is **anathema** to moral people. _____
7. It is easy to explain things to an **obtuse** person. _____
8. Someone with **catholic** views is narrow-minded. _____
9. A large bank account **obviates** financial fears. _____
10. **Erudite** people are well educated. _____

Check your results: 1-F, 2-F, 3-T, 4-T, 5-F, 6-T, 7-F, 8-F, 9-T, 10-T.

THIRD DAY

Test Your Spelling

In a few moments you can find out whether your spelling is as good as it should be, or whether you make errors you're not aware of.

Is Your Spelling as Good as You Are?

Test 7: These ten words baffle many people—do you know how to spell them?

Which is correct, *a* or *b*?

1. (a) drunkeness   (b) drunkenness
2. (a) embarassment   (b) embarrassment
3. (a) all right   (b) alright
4. (a) repetition   (b) repitition
5. (a) occurrance   (b) occurrence
6. (a) occassional   (b) occasional
7. (a) separate   (b) seperate
8. (a) cooly   (b) coolly
9. (a) reccomend   (b) recommend
10. (a) liquefy   (b) liquify

Check your results:

1-b. The adjective **drunken,** plus the ending **-ness.**

2-b. Note that both the r and s are doubled.

3-a. Only the two-word spelling is fully acceptable, no matter what the meaning.

4-a. Think of the verb form **repeat** to remember the correct vowel after the **p.**

5-b. Note the double r and the -ence ending.

6-b. No reason for the double s, though most poor spellers are addicted to it.

7-a. Remember the crucial a by thinking of its synonym, **apart**.

8-b. **Cool** plus the adverbial ending **-ly**.

9-b. The verb **commend**, which everyone spells correctly, plus the prefix **re-**.

10-a. Only five common verbs end in **-efy** rather than the usual **-ify**: liquefy, putrefy, rarefy, stupefy, and of course, **defy**.

Test 8: Do you recognize incorrect spelling?

Find the *single* misspelled word in each line, cross it out, and rewrite it correctly:

1. superintendant, persistent, insistent, dependent, consistent: _____

2. supervise, advertise, despise, analize, memorize: _____

3. dissatisfied, dissimilar, dissapointed, disappear, misspelling, misspent: _____

4. niece, achieve, relieve, recieve, seize, leisure, weird: _____

5. indispensable, irritable, irresistable, dependable, inimitable: _____

Check your results:

1. Change **superintendant** to **superintendent**. These are the five -ent words that are troublesome to insecure spellers. The two most frequently misspelled -ance words are **resistance** and **perseverance**.

2. Change **analize** to **analyze**. The only two common words ending in **-yze** are **analyze** and **paralyze**.

3. Change **dissapointed** to **disappointed**. **Disappointed** and **disappear** are combinations of the prefix **dis-** and the roots **appoint** and **appear**; hence there's no reason for a double s. In the other words, however, the double s is required because the roots start with s: **dis-** plus **satisfied**, **dis-** plus **similar**, **mis-** plus **spelling**, **mis-** plus **spent**.

8

4. Change **recieve** to **receive**. The rule, you will recall, is **i** before **e** except after **c**. Since there is an immediately preceding **c** in **receive**, -**ei**, rather than -ie, is the correct pattern. True, there is no c in **seize, leisure,** and **weird,** but these are the three important exceptions to the rule.

5. Change **irresistable** to **irresistible**. The -**able**, -**ible** problem is one of the thorniest in English spelling, and the five words offered here are the ones that cause the most confusion.

FOURTH DAY

Test Your Grammar

Do you generally use words correctly? Are you usually sure, or only half sure? Let's put it to a test.

Does Your Grammar Make a Good Impression?

No one's grammar is perfect, of course, but conspicuously poor English (such as some of the usages listed below) wrench the listener's attention away from *what* a speaker is saying and direct it to the *error* he is making.

Test 9: Is your English free of glaring errors?

Do some of the following patterns occur with any frequency in your own speech? If you can honestly say "No" (N) in most instances, consider yourself safe. On the other hand, wherever you must admit that you are addicted to a particular error (Y), a little thought and concentration, plus an awareness of the principle involved, can quickly and permanently eliminate the incorrect pattern.

1. He **done**, I **seen** _____
2. **Irregardless** of what you say _____
3. He **don't** like to _____
4. **Him** and **me** can come _____
5. When his mother and father **was** alive _____
6. I **ain't** happy about it _____
7. We **can't hardly** _____
8. I don't need **no** money _____
9. **This here** plan; **that there** statement _____
10. **Them** books, **them** people _____

Check your results:

1. **Done** and **seen** may be used only after **has, have,** or **had**—i.e., in the *perfect tense.* The correct *past tense* of these verbs is **did** and **saw.**
2. The correct word is **regardless**; or, if you prefer to start with a negative prefix, say **irrespective.**
3. **Don't**, a contraction of **do not,** may be used only with a *plural* subject or with the pronoun **I.** Say **doesn't** (a contraction of **does not**) with a *singular* subject: **he doesn't, she doesn't, it doesn't, the man doesn't,** and so forth.
4. **Him** and **me** are objective pronouns—as are **her, us,** and **them**—and may not be used as *subjects* (i.e., before the verb). Say: **He and I** can come.
5. Two words connected by **and** take a *plural* verb: His mother and father **were** alive. The book and pencil **are** hers.
6. While **ain't** is a serviceable word, it is rarely used by educated speakers.
7. **Hardly** and **scarcely** are negative words. When you use them, keep the verb affirmative. Say **can hardly, can scarcely,** etc.
8. Here again the double negative should be avoided. Say: I don't need **any** money. Eliminate the error in these similar sentences: I can't see **no one.** I won't go there **no more.** I didn't take **none.** I didn't talk to **nobody.** I didn't see it **nowhere.**
9. Omit **here** and **there.** Say **this plan, that statement.**
10. **Them** should not be used adjectively. Say **those** or **these.**

Test 10: Are you clear on these points of correct English?

The boldface word in some of the following sentences is used correctly; in others, it violates an established rule of grammar. Do you know which is which? If you can make at least six correct choices (R for *right,* W for *wro*ng), your English is above average.

1. He's not as tall as **me.** _____
2. You work faster than **her.** _____
3. Would you like to visit my brother and **I** tonight? _____
4. If you don't feel well, why don't you **lay** down for a while?

5. He felt so weak that he just **lay** asleep all day. ____
6. Two new schools are now being built, but neither of them **is** finished. ____
7. This is a **most** unique house. ____
8. Let's keep this strictly between you and **me**. ____

Check your results:

1—W. Add the final implied word: He's not as tall as **I** (am).

2—W. As before, if you finish the sentence, you can determine the correct word: You work faster than **she** (does).

3—W. You would say: Visit **me** (*not* **I**)—hence: Visit my brother and **me**. When undecided about a pronoun following **and**, say it over, leaving out the preceding words, and you can't go wrong. For example: He saw (John and) **me** (*not* **I**). We can do without (you and) **her** (*not* **she**). Can you talk to (them and) **us** (*not* **we**)?

4—W. **Lay** means *to place* (something), as: **Lay** the pillow on the bed. When you mean *rest* or *recline*, say **lie**.

5—R. The past tense of **lie** (*to recline* or *rest*) is, strangely enough, **lay**—not **laid** or **lied**. The past of **lay** is **laid**: They **laid** the foundation of the building this morning.

6—R. **Neither of** means *neither one of*, so a singular verb is required. The same rule applies to **either of**.

7—W. **Unique** means *without a like or equal*, so any modifying adjective is superfluous.

8—R. After **between**, which is a preposition, use the *objective* forms of the pronoun: **me, him, her, us, them**. Other prepositions you must learn to be wary of when a pronoun follows, are **except, but** (meaning *except*), **to, with, without, for, from,** and **against**. Study these: No one's here **except us**. Everyone's satisfied **but her**. Will you speak **to** Sam and **me**? May I go **with** you and **him**? We can get along **without** you and **them**.

FIFTH DAY

Just for Fun

Test Your Fluency

How quickly can you call words to mind? Here is a reliable test of your vocabulary responsiveness. In five minutes or less, write next to each of the following words one that starts with **r** and is essentially *opposite* in meaning to, or in contrast with, the given word. Examples: **walk — run, imaginary — real, square — round.**

1. slow
2. common
3. cooked
4. unprepared
5. front
6. forget
7. send
8. increase
9. left
10. green
11. polite
12. transient
13. wholesale
14. submit
15. dull
16. aggressive
17. careful
18. work
19. urban
20. conform

Check your results: 1-rapid; 2-rare; 3-raw; 4-ready; 5-rear; 6-recollect, remember, recall; 7-receive, retain, rescind; 8-reduce, retard; 9-right; 10-red; 11-rude; 12-resident; 13-retail; 14-resist, rebel; 15-radiant; 16-recessive, reticent, retiring, reluctant; 17-reckless; 18-rest, relax(ation), recreation; 19-rural, rustic; 20-resist, rebel.

The Name Behind the Word

boycott: Captain Charles C. Boycott had a run-in with some Irish farmers who refused to pay the exorbitant rents demanded by his company. The Irishmen picketed Boycott's home, refusing to let anyone work for him.

gat: Richard Jordan Gatling invented the machine gun in 1861.

marcel wave: Marcel was a famous French hairdresser who made a fortune out of his new idea in coiffures.

silhouette: Etienne de Silhouette was finance minister of France just before the Revolution. He insisted that the nobles lead *simpler* lives, thus saving money, which of course they could donate to the government. The **silhouette** (as it was later called) was invented at about this time, and was obviously a very *simple* sort of portraiture. The connection of ideas appealed to the Parisian mind, and the minister's name was soon used to describe the new art form.

Did You Know That . . . ?

Italics are so called because this kind of type was first used by an **Italian** printer in Venice.

Drat it is not so mild a curse as it may seem. It is a contraction of **May God rot it.**

Calling an attractive girl a **peach**, far from being modern slang, goes back at least to 1896.

In England a **streetcar** is a **tram**, a **cookie jar** is a **biscuit barrel**, **molasses** is **treacle**, and the **movies** are the **cinema**.

Whiskey is from the Irish *uisgebeatha, water of life.*

Think of Words

Can you think of ten words ending in **-ank**? Add one or two letters only, to fit each definition:

1. _____ank   free from writing, empty
2. _____ank   disagreeably moist
3. _____ank   slender
4. _____ank   noise
5. _____ank   trick
6. _____ank   side of an animal
7. _____ank   an arm for winding
8. _____ank   lower part of the leg
9. _____ank   candid
10. _____ank   board

Now your problem is to think of a word *opposed* in meaning to the definition offered. The initial letter is supplied:

11. a_____   passive
12. b_____   dull
13. c_____   throw
14. d_____   stay
15. e_____   leave
16. f_____   smile
17. g_____   sad
18. h_____   proud
19. i_____   community
20. j_____   senile
21. k_____   be ignorant
22. l_____   stiff
23. m_____   phobia
24. n_____   sophisticated
25. o_____   closed
26. p_____   meek
27. q_____   ordinary
28. r_____   common
29. s_____   complex

30. t_____ wild
31. u_____ unique
32. v_____ valuable
33. w_____ ruddy
34. y_____ white of an egg
35. z_____ lowest point

Check your results: 1-blank; 2-dank; 3-lank; 4-clank; 5-prank; 6-flank; 7-crank; 8-shank; 9-frank; 10-plank; 11-active, alive, alert; 12-bright; 13-catch; 14-depart; 15-enter; 16-frown; 17-gay, glad; 18-humble; 19-individual; 20-juvenile; 21-know; 22-lithe, lax; 23-mania; 24-naïve; 25-open(ed); 26-proud; 27-quaint, queer; 28-rare; 29-simple; 30-tame; 31-universal; 32-valueless; 33-wan, white; 34-yolk, yellow; 35-zenith.

PART II

Say It Right

"Art thou an Ephraimite?"
"Nay."
"Say now the word for an ear of corn."
"Sibboleth."

This is undoubtedly the earliest recorded instance of a pronunciation quiz. It was administered in Biblical times (you will find an account of it in the Book of Judges) by a Gileadite who caught a suspected Ephraimite trying to cross the river Jordan. The prisoner vowed he was a Gileadite, but his pronunciation gave him away. Gileadites called an ear of corn **shibboleth,** not **sibboleth.** This error generally cost an Ephraimite his life—a harsh penalty for a single mispronunciation.

Times have not changed as much as you may think. During World War II, a Japanese soldier who claimed to be Chinese or Filipino was given a quick pronunciation test by his American captors: he was asked to say **lalapalooza.** To the Japanese ear, **l** is an unpronounceable sound; so if the prisoner was not what he pretended to be, the best he could manage was **raraparooza**. He had flunked the test; his pronunciation had given him away!

The importance of correct pronunciation to *your* life, though probably never so crucial as to threaten your continued existence or even your freedom, should not be minimized. From your pronunciation—especially of certain common and frequently used English words—people form their first impressions of your educational background, of your ability and intelligence, perhaps even of your personality. This is unfortunate and in many instances probably illogical, for what a person says is certainly a much more reliable criterion of his worth than how he says it. But human nature is not always reasonable, and listeners tend to jump to sweeping conclusions about you from the way you speak.

Your pronunciation, therefore, either adds to or detracts from the power and persuasiveness of your ideas. And since the effectiveness of a spoken thought stems not only from the thought itself or from the words in which it is expressed, but also—often even more so—from the self-assurance of the speaker, your own confidence in your pronunciation can be an important factor in helping you put across your ideas successfully. So the following chapters have these aims:

• To give you practical training in pronouncing correctly some of the most troublesome words in the English language.
• To offer you practice in these words, so that correct pronunciation becomes habitual and completely natural.
• To root out of your speech, permanently and completely, every possibility of unconscious error.
• To settle any doubts or confusion you may have about certain pronunciation demons.
• To increase your self-assurance in expressing your ideas **and thoughts.**

SIXTH DAY

Practice in Pronunciation

Can you pass this easy pronunciation test?

Your reaction to these nine significant English words will tell you a great deal about your pronunciation habits:

1. radiator
2. mischievous
3. genuine
4. comparable
5. chiropodist
6. human
7. influence
8. accessory
9. gesture

Test Your Pronunciation

High on the list of troublesome words are nine demons that have a diabolical ability to trap the unwary speaker. How do you pronounce each one? Make your decision *not* on the basis of what you may think is correct, but solely on the basis of what you would say in ordinary conversation.

> The symbol ə indicates the very slight vowel sound heard in the first syllable of **commit** (kə-MIT′) or the last syllable of **Linda** (LIN′-də).

1. **radiator:** (a) RAD′-ee-ay-tər; (b) RAY′-dee-ay-tər
2. **mischievous:** (a) miss-CHEE′-vee-əs; (b) MISS′-chə-ves
3. **genuine:** (a) JEN′-yoo-in; (b) JEN′-yoo-wine
4. **comparable:** (a) KOM′-pə-rə-bel; (b) kəm-PAR′-ə-bəl (AR as in *carriage*)

19

5. **chiropodist:** (a) kə-ROP′-ə-dist; (b) tchə-ROP′-ə-dist
6. **human:** (a) YOO′-mən; (b) HYOO′-mən
7. **influence:** (a) in-FLOO′-əncе; (b) IN′-floo-əncе
8. **accessory:** (a) a-SESS′-ər-ee; (b) ak-SESS′-ər-ee
9. **gesture:** (a) JES′-chər; (b) GES′-chər (g as in *get*)

Check your results: 1-b, 2-b, 3-a, 4-a, 5-a, 6-b, 7-b, 8-b, 9-a.

Say It Aloud

Knowing the correct forms is only half the battle in your conquest of pronunciation demons. The other, and possibly more important, half is developing the habit of *using* the correct forms without hesitation whenever you speak. An awareness that the first **a** of **radiator** is pronounced as it is in **bay**, or that **mischievous** has three syllables rather than four, is of little benefit if you still unthinkingly say RAD′-ee-ay-tər and miss-CHEE′-vee-əs in your everyday conversation. Only practice will permanently root these mispronunciations out of your speech. So say these words aloud several times, hear them correctly in your own voice, push them deep into your consciousness:

1. **radiator:** RAY′-dee-ay-tər
2. **mischievous:** MISS′-chə-vəs
3. **genuine:** JEN′-yoo-in
4. **comparable:** KOM′-pə-rə-bəl
5. **chiropodist:** kə-ROP′-ə-dist
6. **human:** HYOO′-mən
7. **influence:** IN′-floo-əncе
8. **accessory:** ak-SESS′-ər-ee
9. **gesture:** JES′-chər

So far you have been practicing the correct sounds of these tricky demons with a proper wariness and a certain self-consciousness. Suppose you were uttering them casually in conversation: would you unhesitatingly avoid the pitfalls? Let us see. Read these phrases aloud, quickly and naturally—and, of course, correctly: *a hot radiator; human mischievousness; great influence; incomparably skillful chiropodist; a funny gesture; optional accessories.*

Watch Your Accent

Each of the nine words covered up to this point serves as a warning sign of a kind of error effective speakers have learned to avoid.

Comparable, for example, is one of a group of demons ending in **-able** that cause the most plaguing type of accent trouble. Your final and complete conquest of this group will require patience and tenacity. Accenting the indicated syllable may at first seem almost superhumanly difficult; but it will become gradually easier with practice. Listen to yourself carefully, or ask a friend to listen to you, as you say the following words aloud. Make sure you are accenting the capitalized syllable—not the one after it:

1. COM'-parable
2. PREF'-erable
3. AM'-icable
4. HOS'-pitable
5. AD'-mirable
6. LAM'-entable
7. EX'-plicable
8. AP'-plicable
9. FOR'midable
10. REP'-utable
11. DES'-picable

In other forms of these words, the accent remains on the same syllable: in-COM'-parable, in-HOS'-pitable, dis-REP'-utable, COM'-parability, and so forth.

When you are sure you have all these words under effortless control, try reading these phrases aloud and see if you can, without difficulty, keep the accent where it belongs: *admirable results; amicable settlement; lamentable error; despicable dishonesty; applicable examples.*

SEVENTH DAY

More Practice in Good Pronunciation

Here are twenty-five important words that poor speakers say in a slovenly fashion. How about you?

Say It Clearly

Now let us look at another group of pronunciation demons: words, like **accessory**, that may tempt unwary speakers into omitting essential letters. This leads to the kind of slovenly articulation that robs speech of forcefulness. Say each word aloud with particular attention to the italicized letter, which should be sounded distinctly:

1. ac*c*essory: ak-SESS'-ər-ee
2. suc*c*inct: sək-SINGKT'
3. ac*c*ept: ak-SEPT'
4. ac*c*ede: ak-SEED'
5. ac*c*elerator: ak-SEL'-ə-ray-tər
6. lib*r*ary: LYE'-brer-ee
7. Feb*r*uary: FEB'-roo-er-ee
8. leng*t*h: LENGKTH
9. streng*t*h: STRENGKTH
10. wi*d*th: WIDTH
11. gover*n*ment: GUV'-ərn-mənt
12. *g*eography: jee-OG'-rə-fee
13. *e*leven: ə-LEV'-ən
14. as*k*ed: ASKT
15. pi*c*ture: PIK'-chər
16. proba*b*ly: PROB'-əb-lee
17. ru*i*n (2 syllables): ROO'-ən

18. **poem** (2 syllables): PO'-əm
19. **recognize**: REK'-əg-nize
20. **particular**: pər-TIK'-yə-lər
21. **figure**: FIG'-yər
22. **regular**: REG'-yə-lər
23. **accurate**: AK'-yə-rət
24. **manufacture**: man-yə-FAK'-chər
25. **kept**: KEPT

In this type of word especially, only constant repetition of the correct form is likely to be effective in changing habits. So be relentless in your practice; read the entire list *aloud* as often as you think necessary to engrave the crucial letter of each word on your mind. Then check on the success of your practice by reading the following phrases quickly, to see if you are saying all the sounds that should be heard: *succinct and acceptable analysis; length and width of the library; February the eleventh; recognized the government; kept the picture; accurate figures; regular manufactures; of particular strength; probably ruined the poem; asked for geography.*

Let us now cruise along over the remaining categories, with the understanding that final and complete mastery can be achieved only from repeated practice. Single out for special attention those groups in which you feel weakest, and be generous with your time and effort. Frequent repetition of the words *aloud* will make correct habits so deep-seated that the possibility of error, even in the heat of animated conversation, will be reduced to the vanishing point.

Don't Say Too Much

In the previous section, your practice was devoted to words in which speakers often casually ignore essential letters that should be clearly pronounced. This section, on the contrary, offers the kind of demon—**mischievous** is a typical example—in which some people tend to insert sounds that aren't there.

Read each word in column 1 aloud. Check your pronunciation by referring to the correct form in column 2. Are you saying no more than necessary? Make sure that you avoid the incorrect form listed in column 3.

1.	mischievous	MISS'-chə-vəs	miss-CHEE'-vee-əs
2.	grievous	GREE'-vəs	GREE'-vee-əs
3.	film	FILM (1 syllable)	FILL'-əm
4.	elm	ELM (1 syllable)	ELL'-əm
5.	drowned	DROWND (1 syllable)	DROWN'-ded
6.	percolator	PUR'-kə-lay-tər	PUR'-kyə-lay-tər
7.	attacked	ə-TAKT'	ə-TAK'-təd
8.	athletic	ath-LET'-ic	ath-ə-LET'-ic
9.	athlete	ATH'-leet	ATH'-ə-leet

Sound Your h

In a few English words, such as **honor** and **honest**, the letter h is, of course, silent; but in the following words, the **h** should be clearly pronounced. Try these aloud:

1. *h*uman
2. *h*umanity
3. *h*umane
4. *h*umor
5. *h*umorous
6. *h*umid
7. *h*umidity
8. *h*uge
9. *h*umble
10. *h*omage

In **herb**, the h is usually silent, but it is equally correct to sound it: say either **'erb** or **herb**.

Beware of g

The letter g is tricky and confusing. Often it is hard, as in **game**. Just as often, especially before **e, i,** and **y**, it is soft, as in **gem, gin,** and **gymnasium**.

24

Beware particularly of the following words, in each of which g is soft, with the sound of **j**:

1. mangy
2. gesture
3. gesticulate
4. turgid
5. intelligentsia
6. gibberish
7. gibe
8. longevity (lon-JEV'-ə-tee)

And beware, too, of these, in which **g** has the same sound as the **s** in **pleasure, treasure,** or **measure,** indicated usually by the symbol **zh.** Say **pleasure** several times aloud, noting the characteristic sound of the **s;** then give the same sound to **g** in each of the following:

1. **garage:** gə-RAHZH'
2. **barrage:** bə-RAHZH'
3. **camouflage:** KAM'-ə-flahzh
4. **massage:** mə-SAHZH'
5. **corsage:** kor-SAHZH'
6. **sabotage:** SAB'-ə-tahzh
7. **prestige:** press-TEEZH'
8. **cortege:** kor-TEZH'

Practice aloud with an alert ear, to make sure you are *not* pronouncing the **g** like a **j.** The tongue should hang slack in the mouth rather than hit the front of the palate, and the result should be fairly liquid.

Keep Sounds Untwisted

In eight special words, poor speakers tend to transpose sounds, pronouncing them in incorrect order, often with humorous results. Try these:

1. **bronchial:** BRONG'-kee-əl — not BRON'-ə-kəl (Note that ch precedes the i.)
2. **superfluous:** soo-PUR'-floo-əs — not soo-PUR'-fə-ləs (Note that l precedes the u.)
3. **larynx:** LAR'-inx (a as in *hat*) — not LAHR'-nix (Note that y precedes the n.)
4. **irrelevant:** ir-REL'-ə-vənt — not ir-REV'-ə-lənt (Note that l precedes the v.)

5. **modern:** MOD′-ərn — not MOD′-rən (Note that e precedes the **r**.)
6. **pattern:** PAT′-ərn — not PAT′-rən (Note again that **e** precedes the **r**.)
7. **perspiration:** pur-spə-RAY′-shən — not press-pə-RAY′-shən (Note that **e** precedes the **r**.)
8. **prescription:** prə-SKRIP′-shən — not pər-SKRIP′-shən (Note that in this word, on the other hand, **r** precedes the **e**.)

Get Straight on -ile

Most words that end in **-ile** are preferably pronounced with the ending **-ill**, to rhyme with **mill**, with the exceptions noted later. Practice the following by saying them aloud over and over again:

1. **fragile:** FRAJ′-ill
2. **servile:** SUR′-vill
3. **versatile:** VUR′-sə-till
4. **fertile:** FUR′-till
5. **imbecile:** IM′-bə-sill
6. **hostile:** HOS′-till
7. **sterile:** STER′-ill
8. **docile:** DOSS′-ill
9. **agile:** AJ′-ill
10. **futile:** FYOO′-till
11. **virile:** VIR′-ill
    (not VER′-ill)

In these exceptions, the last syllable rhymes with **mile**:

1. **infantile:** IN′-fən-tile
2. **senile:** SEE′-nile
3. **profile:** PRO′-file
4. **exile:** EK′-sile or EG′-zile
5. **reconcile:** REK′-ən-sile
6. **crocodile:** KROK′-ə-dile
7. **turnstile:** TURN′-stile
8. **bibliophile:** BIB′-lee-ə-file

In four special words, you may rhyme the ending either with **mill** or with **mile**, whichever sounds better to you:

1. juvenile
2. textile
3. mercantile
4. domicile

EIGHTH DAY
Still More Words That Fool the Unwary

Examine four final categories of English words; then check the success of your learning in Part II by taking a test that most unsophisticated speakers would do very poorly on.

Don't Misplace Accents

The position of the accent in English words is more often a stumbling block and a source of doubt and confusion than any other single factor. Here are twenty troublemakers:

1. **banquet:** BANG'-kwət
2. **impious:** IM'-pee-əs
3. **infamous:** IN'-fə-məs
4. **influence:** IN'-floo-ənce
5. **distribute:** dis-TRIB'-yət
6. **affluence:** AF'-floo-ənce
7. **awry:** ə-RYE'
8. **remonstrate:** rə-MON'-strate
9. **deficit:** DEF'-ə-sit
10. **champion:** CHAM'-pee-ən
11. **integral:** IN'-tə-grəl
12. **municipal:** myoo-NISS'-ə-pəl
13. **intricate:** IN'-trə-kit
14. **intricacy:** IN'-trə-kə-see
15. **caricature:** KĂR'-ə-kə-choor (ĂR as in *carriage*)
16. **robust:** rə-BUST'
17. **acumen:** ə-KYOO'-mən
18. **plebeian:** plə-BEE'-ən
19. **ignominious:** ig-ne-MIN'-ee-əs
20. **dirigible:** DIR'-ə-jə-bəl

27

In the following eight words you have greater freedom in placing the accent:

1. exquisite: EX'-kwi-zit or ex-KWIZ'-it
2. adult: ə-DULT' or AD'-ult
3. inquiry: in-KWY'-ree or IN'-kwə-ree
4. aspirant: as-PIRE'-ənt or ASS'-pi-rənt
5. incognito: in-KOG'-nə-tō or in-cog-NEE'-tō (o as in *go*)
6. secretive: sə-KREE'-tiv or SEEK'-rə-tiv
7. acclimate: ə-KLY'-mət or AK'-lə-mayt
8. address, as in *name and address:* ə-DRESS' or AD'-dress; as a verb, or with other meanings: ə-DRESS' only

Don't Be Misled by ch

Chiropodist, you have learned, starts with the sound of **k,** despite the spelling **ch.** In the following words the deceptive **ch** is also pronounced as a **k:**

1. chasm: KAZ'-əm
2. machinations: mak-ə-NAY'-shənz
3. chaos: KAY'-oss
4. archipelago: ahr-kə-PEL'-ə-go

Get Straight on a's

In **radiator,** as you now know, the first syllable rhymes with **bay:** RAY'-dee-ay-tər. The same is true of **aviator** (AY'-vee-ay-tər) and **verbatim** (vər-BAY'-təm). But in the following nine words you may use either the **a** of **bay** or of **hat:**

1. **data:** DAY'-tə or DAT'-ə
2. **status:** STAY'-təs or STAT'-əs
3. **fracas:** FRAY'-kəs or FRAK'-əs
4. **ignoramus:** ig-nə-RAY'-mə or ig-nə-RAM'-əs
5. **ultimatum:** ul-tə-MAY'-təm or ul-tə-MAT'-əm
6. **strata:** STRAY'-tə or STRAT'-ə
7. **pro rata:** pro RAY'-tə or pro RAT'-ə
8. **gratis:** GRAY'-təs or GRAT'-əs
9. **apparatus:** ap-ə-RAY'-təs or ap-ə-RAT'-əs

Speak Unaffectedly

Here is a final group of seven words in which the choice of pronunciation is a source of uncertainty to many students. The first pronunciation listed is recommended because it is popular, inconspicuous, unaffected—and therefore safe. On the other hand, the second form is prevalent in some sections of the country. Use it if your instinctive preference inclines you strongly in that direction and if you are quite sure your pronunciation will not set you apart from those with whom you usually talk:

		Recommended	*Less Widely Used*
1.	either	EE'-thər	EYE'-thər
2.	neither	NEE'-thər	NYE'-thər
3.	aunt	ANT	AHNT
4.	vase	VAYZ or VAYS	VAHZ
5.	tomato	tə-MAY'-tō	tə-MAH'-tō (ō as in *go*)
6.	rather	RA'-thər (rhymes with *gather*)	RAH'-thər (rhymes with *father*)
7.	chauffeur	SHO'-fər	shə-FUR'

Test Your Learning

We have thoroughly explored twelve categories of demons that are the most devilish and the most troublesome in the entire English language. These words, more than any others, create doubt and confusion.

If you have worked on Part II, if you have begun to form new habits through repeated practice, then these words are no longer demons for you. They are no longer a source of possible error—no longer a cause of anxiety or lack of self-confidence.

Let us put the results of your study to a test. Here is a representative sampling of the words covered in Part II. Are you able now, unhesitatingly and unerringly, to make a correct choice?

1. **genuine:** (a) JEN'-yoo-wine; (b) JEN'-yoo-in
2. **manufacture:** (a) man-ə-FAK'-chər'; (b) man-yə-FAK'-cher
3. **preferable:** (a) PREF'-ər-ə-bəl; (b) prə-FER'-ə-bəl
4. **figure:** (a) FIG'-ər; (b) FIG'-yər
5. **grievous:** (a) GREE'-vəs; (b) GREE'-vee-əs
6. **athletic:** (a) ath-ə-LET'-ic; (b) ath-LET'-ic
7. **huge:** (a) HYOOJ; (b) YOOJ
8. **gesture:** (a) GES'-chər; (b) JES'-chər
9. **prestige:** (a) press-TEEZH; (b) press-TEEDJ'
10. **bronchial:** (a) BRON'-ə-kəl; (b) BRONG'-kee-əl
11. **fertile:** (a) FUR'-till; (b) FUR'-tile
12. **senile:** (a) SEN'-ill; (b) SEE'-nile
13. **impious:** (a) IM'-pee-əs' (b) im-PY'-əs
14. **awry:** (a) ə-RYE'; (b) AW'-ree
15. **intricacy:** (a) in-TRIK'-ə-see; (b) IN'-trə-kə-see
16. **dirigible:** (a) DIR'-ə-jə-bəl; (b) də-RIJ'-ə-bəl
17. **machinations:** (a) mak-ə-NAY'-shənz; (b) match-ə-NAY'-shənz
18. **aviator:** (a) AV'-ee-ay-tər; (b) AY'-vee-ty-tər

Check your results: 1-b, 2-b, 3-a, 4-b, 5-a, 6-b, 7-a, 8-b, 9-a, 10-b, 11-a, 12-b, 13-a, 14-a, 15-b, 16-a, 17-a, 18-b.

NINTH DAY

Just for Fun

It's Murder!

Killing anyone is generally illegal, usually unethical, and almost always unpleasant. But murder goes back at least as far as Cain and Abel, and even in the most civilized of countries it is always part of the current scene.

Here are ten of the most popular victims of murder in one column, and the words that identify the type of killing in another column. How successfully can you match the word to the deed?

1. whole groups or races of people
2. one's mother
3. one's father
4. one's brother
5. one's sister
6. either parent, or anyone in a parental capacity
7. one's king
8. any human being
9. one's wife
10. worms, especially the intestinal, parasitic variety

(a) **sororicide**
(b) **uxoricide**
(c) **vermicide**
(d) **homicide**
(e) **parricide**
(f) **fratricide**
(g) **genocide**
(h) **patricide**
(i) **regicide**
(j) **matricide**

Check your results: 1-g, 2-j, 3-h, 4-f, 5-a, 6-e, 7-i, 8-d, 9-b, 10-c.

Illogical Expressions

Isn't it odd how some words don't always mean what they seem to say? For example:

Commencement comes at the end of a college course.
We **sail** to Europe by **steamship**.
A seaplane **lands** on **water**.
A hospital is **manned** by **women**.
What was in yesterday's paper is **old news**.
Something grows smaller.

The Thirteen Words Most Often Mispronounced

There are hundreds of thousands of words in our language, and though few of us know or use all of them, it is likely that thousands of different ones pass our lips in a week's conversation.

Here's what is startling: out of these thousands of words in daily use, *exactly thirteen* are more frequently mispronounced by the average speaker than any other words, common or uncommon, in the entire English language.

This statistic has been discovered through investigations made in vocabulary-improvement classes in the Division of General Education of New York University. Term after term, with different students, the result is confirmed: it's always the same thirteen words that cause the most trouble.

You will find this most-sinned-against baker's dozen of English words directly below—and a chance to find out whether you tend to make the same mistakes as most other people. Check the pronunciation you honestly and habitually use; then compare your results with the key below. If you're average, you should get no more than four or five right; six to eight correct choices will indicate a high degree of linguistic sophistication; nine to twelve will mean that your command of English is remarkable; and a perfect score will mark you as unique, no less.

1. **manufacture:** (a) man-yə-FAK'-chər; (b) man-ə-FAK'-char
2. **human:** (a) YOO'-mən; (b) HYOO'-mən
3. **forte** (*strong point*): (a) FOR'-tay; (b) FORT
4. **genuine:** (a) JEN'-yoo-win; (b) JEN'-yoo-wine
5. **acumen** (mental keenness): (a) ə-KYOO'-mən; (b) AK'-yoo-mən
6. **admirable:** (a) ad-MIRE'-ə-bəl; (b) AD'-mə-rə-bəl
7. **mischievous:** (a) mis-CHEE'-vee-əs; (b) MIS'-chə-vəs
8. **radiator:** (a) RAY'-dee-ay-tər; (b) RAD'-ee-ay-tər
9. **grimace** (*facial contortion*): (a) grə-MAYCE'; (b) GRIM'-əss
10. **impious** (*against religion*): (a) im-PYE'-əs; (b) IM'-pee-əs
11. **finis** (*the end*): (a) fee-NEE'; (b) FIN'-iss; (c) FYE'-niss
12. **naïveté** (*artlessness*): (a) NAY'-və-tee; (b) nah-eev-TAY'; (c) nay-VET'
13. **integral** (*essential*): (a) IN'-tə-grəl; (b) in-TEG'-rəl; (c) in-TEE'-grəl

Check your results: 1-a, 2-b, 3-b, 4-a, 5-a, 6-b, 7-b, 8-a, 9-a, 10-b, 11-c, 12-b, 13-a.

What Kind of Speller Are You?

English spelling is no cinch, and the ten demons below may throw you if you don't keep an eye peeled. Check the pattern you trust; then see below for answers.

1. (a) embarrassing; (b) embarassing; (c) embarrasing
2. (a) superintendent; (b) superintendant
3. (a) catagory; (b) category
4. (a) supercede; (b) superceed; (c) supersede
5. (a) annoint; (b) anoint
6. (a) absence; (b) abscence
7. (a) occurance; (b) occurrence; (c) occurence
8. (a) exhillarate; (b) exhilirate; (c) exhilarate
9. (a) dispair; (b) despair
10. (a) dissipate; (b) dissapate; (c) disippate

33

Check your results: 1-a, 2-a, 3-b, 4-c, 5-b, 6-a, 7-b, 8-c, 9-b, 10-a.

See Part IV for special tricks to improve your spelling.

PART III

Improve Your Vocabulary

Vocabulary is important. Success—in school, and later in professional and business life—has an eminently logical connection with the number of words one knows and can recognize and use. So now let's get down to some intensive work in vocabulary building.

TENTH DAY

A Simple Program for Vocabulary Improvement

To increase your vocabulary at a prodigious rate, you must learn to be on the alert for new words.

Children Learn Words Faster Than You Do!

Words are the tools of thinking, of understanding, of self-expression. It would therefore be nice to conclude that the older you get, the faster your vocabulary keeps growing and the faster you amass verbal tools for thinking accurately and for expressing yourself clearly and effectively. Such a conclusion, if applied to the average adult, would unfortunately be entirely wrong.

Carefully controlled investigations by Professor Robert H. Seashore, Chairman of the Department of Psychology of Northwestern University, show that children between the ages of four and ten increase their vocabularies at a prodigious rate as compared with most adults who have completed their formal education.

A child of ten usually has a vocabulary of thirty thousand words, according to Professor Seashore, and has been learning new words at the rate of *several thousand a year*. Contrast these figures with those gathered by testing thousands of noncollege adults taking vocabulary courses in the Division of General Education of New York University: the average adult vocabulary is about fifty thousand words (roughly two thirds bigger than that of a child of ten), and the steady increase made by adults after leaving school is rarely more than twenty-five new words a year!

Johnson O'Connor, director of the Human Engineering Laboratory, an institution that tests the aptitudes and vocabularies of thousands of adults yearly, reports the same results: "From [age] twenty-three to fifty, vocabulary continues to increase, *but changes no more in these twenty-five years than in two school years."* (Italics added.)

If you feel that your own vocabulary has come almost to a standstill, you may wonder what you can do about it.

You can do a great deal. Although you might normally, and without conscious effort, learn twenty-five new words in a twelve-month period, you can, in just the brief time it will take you to complete the work of this tenth day, add as many as sixty-seven new words to your vocabulary—more than the average person learns in two full years!

Vocabulary Is Important

Before proceeding with the learning of new words, let us consider for a moment the importance of a good vocabulary.

In our modern world, the person with a good vocabulary has a better chance of success. This is true not only in his school career, but also when he gets into the business or professional world.

Let us take a look at just a small amount of the evidence that points to this intimate relationship between vocabulary and scholastic, business, and professional success.

At the University of Illinois, entering students are routinely given a short vocabulary test. From the results, it has been found that an accurate prediction can be made of probable academic success—or lack of success—over the entire four-year college course.

The Human Engineering Laboratory tested the vocabularies of one hundred young men in the graduating class of the business school of a large university. Five years later, a survey of the careers of those one hundred students revealed this spectacular pair of statistics: (1) every senior who had scored in the upper 10 per cent of the group had become an executive; (2) not a single young man whose score was in the lowest 25 per cent had attained an executive position.

Further, the Laboratory, after testing the vocabularies of thousands of people in all age groups and in all walks of life, found that *the only common characteristic of successful people in this country was an unusual grasp of the meanings of words.*

Now, in Part III of this book, you have an opportunity to check the quality of your vocabulary, and then to do something about improving it.

Take This Vocabulary Test

You are probably curious to learn how your own vocabulary stacks up against that of other people. To find out, take this simple ten-minute test.

Below are twenty-five phrases, each containing a word in boldface type. Check what you consider to be the correct definition of every word with which you have any familiarity, however slight; omit an answer, however, if the boldface word is totally unfamiliar:

1. **disheveled** appearance: (a) untidy; (b) fierce; (c) foolish; (d) unhappy
2. a **baffling** problem: (a) difficult; (b) simple; (c) puzzling; (d) old; (e) new
3. extremely **lenient** parents: (a) tall; (b) not strict; (c) wise; (d) neglectful; (e) severe
4. an **audacious** attempt: (a) useless; (b) bold; (c) unwise; (d) crazy; (e) necessary

5. **agile** climber: (a) lively; (b) tired; (c) skillful; (d) careful; (e) fast

6. **prevalent** disease: (a) dangerous; (b) catching; (c) childhood; (d) fatal; (e) widespread

7. **ominous** report: (a) loud; (b) threatening; (c) untrue; (d) serious; (e) unpleasant

8. an **incredible** story: (a) true; (b) interesting; (c) well-known; (d) unbelievable; (e) unknown

9. will **supersede** the old law: (a) enforce; (b) specify penalties for; (c) take the place of; (d) repeal; (e) continue in force

10. an **anonymous** donor: (a) generous; (b) stingy; (c) considerate; (d) one whose name is not known; (e) reluctant

11. an **indefatigable** worker: (a) well-paid; (b) conscientious; (c) courteous; (d) tireless; (e) pleasant

12. a **loquacious** woman: (a) motherly; (b) attractive; (c) homely; (d) seductive; (e) talkative

13. living in **affluence**: (a) filth; (b) countrified surroundings; (c) fear; (d) wealth; (e) poverty

14. to **simulate** interest: (a) pretend; (b) feel; (c) lose; (d) stir up; (e) ask for

15. a **congenital** deformity: (a) disfiguring; (b) crippling; (c) slight; (d) incurable; (e) occurring at or during birth

16. took an **unequivocal** stand: (a) indecisive; (b) unexplainable; (c) unexpected; (d) definite; (e) hard to understand

17. **vicarious** enjoyment: (a) complete; (b) unspoiled; (c) occurring from a feeling of identification with another; (d) long-continuing; (e) temporary

18. **anachronous** garb: (a) absurd; (b) religious; (c) belonging to a different time; (d) out of place; (e) unusual

19. his **iconoclastic** phase: (a) artistic; (b) sneering at tradition; (c) troubled; (d) juvenile; (e) emotional

20. **semantic** confusion: (a) relating to the meanings of words; (b) relating to hearing; (c) relating to emotions; (d) relating to mathematics; (e) relating to vision

21. **cavalier** treatment: (a) polite; (b) highhanded; (c) negligent; (d) incomplete; (e) expensive

22. an **anomalous** situation: (a) dangerous; (b) intriguing; (c) uncommon; (d) pleasant; (e) tragic

23. his **laconic** reply: (a) immediate; (b) truthful; (c) terse and meaningful; (d) unintelligible; (e) angry

24. an unusually **gregarious** person: (a) calm; (b) company-loving; (c) untrustworthy; (d) vicious; (e) self-sacrificing

25. the **cacophony** of the city: (a) political administration; (b) crowded living conditions; (c) cultural advantages; (d) harsh sounds; (e) foul odors

Check your results: 1-a, 2-c, 3-b, 4-b, 5-a, 6-e, 7-b, 8-d, 9-c, 10-d, 11-d, 12-e, 13-d, 14-a, 15-e, 16-d, 17-c, 18-c, 19-b, 20-a, 21-b, 22-c, 23-c, 24-b, 25-d.

How to Make New Words Come Alive

Learning new words is a lot easier than you may think—provided you go about it in the right way. One of the secrets of successful vocabulary building is *repetition*.

To add a new word to your vocabulary so that it really sticks there—permanently, unforgettably, usefully—you must see or hear that word in many different contexts and in a variety of different forms.

Your first contact with a new word will be a fuzzy one. You will see in it no more than a meaningless pattern of syllables, a lifeless collection of letters. But at each successive contact, if the word is an integral part of a sentence, an idea, a thought, you will feel more and more life in the once dead syllables, until finally you will be able to make an instantaneous mental reaction every time you read the word in a page of print or hear it from somebody's lips.

You will then have taken the first crucial step toward getting on friendly terms with a new word; you will have made it part of your *recognition vocabulary*.

Your attitude toward the word has thus far been a passive one. But you must also develop an active attitude. You must begin to use the word. You must learn to call it forth from the recesses of your recognition vocabulary whenever, in thinking, speaking, or writing, you have a use for it. You must, in short, add it to your *functional vocabulary*.

Here are the steps that will help you do all these things:

Consider each new word a challenge. There is always a great temptation to ignore an unfamiliar word that you meet in your reading—to skip over it quickly and blindly if you can manage to extract some meaning, however slight, from the sentence or paragraph in which it occurs. *Resist this temptation.* Consider a new word a red light, a stop sign, a challenge to your imagination and ingenuity. Look at it, become familiar with its appearance, puzzle out its possible meaning from the context.

Try this now: Here are eight words that may be new to you. They are admittedly not everyday terms, and they are fairly complex in meaning; indeed they have been chosen for these very qualities. Examine the sentence fragment in which each word appears, arrive at a probable or possible meaning, even make a wild guess if you wish—but at least come to grips with the challenge with which each of the words will confront you:

1. felt so listless, so completely **enervated**: (a) weakened; (b) tired; (c) confused; (d) defeated

2. such contemptible **sycophancy**: (a) insincere virtuousness; (b) self-seeking flattery; (c) pretense at genuineness; (d) sneakiness and spying

3. no organic disease, but a kind of persistent **hypochondria**: (a) illness of psychological origin; (b) morbid fancies that one is ill, though physically healthy; (c) attitude of unhealthy fear; (d) state of mental delusions

4. so withdrawn and **introverted** as to seem positively unsociable; (a) preferring solitude to the company of others; (b) insulting and hostile in conversation; (c) morbidly silent; (d) more

41

interested in one's thoughts, feelings, etc., than in the outside world

5. such outspoken **misogyny** as to alienate, if not repel, all women: (a) fear of women; (b) hatred of women; (c) pursuit of women; (d) discourtesy to women

6. her **altruistic** generosity: (a) showing more oncern for the welfare of others than for one's own; (b) unlimited; (c) pretended and insincere; (d) well-advertised

7. his name, which is **anathema** to all patriots: (a) an object of speculation; (b) an object of the deepest loathing; (c) an object of respect and devotion; (d) an example of true and unselfish loyalty

8. **disparaged** every attempt he made: (a) blocked; (b) supported; (c) criticized; (d) belittled

Check up on your response to the challenge. You have here been offered a choice of possible meanings for each of the boldface words. In your own efforts, of course, you will think of one or more possibilities by yourself. As you puzzle out each word in the context in which you find it, your guesses may be correct, they may be close though not absolutely exact, or they may be far, far afield. No matter. You're working with the word, you're thinking about it, you're developing a mindset that gives the new word an unobstructed entry into your recognition vocabulary. Having done this, your next and obvious step is to refer to a good dictionary to check up on your success in figuring out meanings. For valuable practice, make such reference to a dictionary at this very moment in respect to the eight words, to see how well you figured out their meanings. (A key to this exercise is deliberately omitted.)

Practice pronouncing and spelling each word. Now you have the word in front of you in the dictionary. You see its pronounciation. You are getting a second visual impression of its appearance. And you will note that it may have other forms for use as different parts of speech (adjective, noun, verb, etc.). Say the word (and any of its derivative forms) aloud. Get accustomed to hearing it in your own voice. Write the word once or twice, so that you will be reacting to it muscularly as well as visually and vocally. These activities will be a giant step in getting on such good terms with the word that it can easily pass into your functional vocabulary and be ready for immediate use when the occasion occurs.

1. **enervated** (enervating, to enervate, enervation)
2. **sycophancy** (sycophantic, a sycophant)
3. **hypochondria** (hypochondriacal, a hypochondriac)
4. **introverted** (introversion, an introvert)
5. **misogyny** (misogynous, misognist)
6. **altruistic** (altruism, an altruist)
7. **anathema** (to anathematize, anathematization)
8. **to disparage** (disparagement, disparaging)

Just three simple steps to add a new word to your recognition and functional vocabulary:

- Keep a sharp eye open to its first appearance, and in meeting it, puzzle out a possible meaning.
- Look it up to determine how successfully you reacted to it.
- Practice saying it aloud and writing it.

Do this as time and circumstances and your reading habits make possible, and you will be truly amazed at how many words will enter your vocabulary almost every day; how you will become more and more aware of their deeper meanings and various forms and uses as you continue meeting them in your reading; how you will become so familiar with them that, practically without being aware of it, you will start to use them in your thinking, your speaking, and your writing.

Do not accept these promises on faith; learn how true they

are from your own experience. Here are three more tests to make these eight words come fully alive for you, to nail them down in your vocabulary, to make them integral factors in your thinking, understanding, and self-expression.

Test 1: True or false?

Decide whether the following statements are substantially *true* (T) or *false* (F):

1. Staying up all night can be **enervating**. ____
2. **Sycophants** seek to curry favor with people of influence or wealth. ____
3. A **hypochondriac's** ailment can be readily discovered through a physical checkup. ____
4. An **introvert** is more interested in other people than in himself. ____
5. A **misogynist** enjoys the company of women. ____
6. **Altruistic** people are often well liked. ____
7. Communism is **anathema** to loyal Americans. ____
8. A **disparaging** remark is intended to express the speaker's praise. ____

Check your results: 1-T, 2-T, 3-F, 4-F, 5-F, 6-T, 7-T, 8-F.

Test 2: Same or opposite?

Decide whether the paired words or phrases are more nearly the *same* (S) or more nearly *opposed* (O) in meaning:

1. **enervate:** strengthen ____
2. **sycophant:** enemy ____
3. **hypochondriac:** realist ____
4. **introvert:** self-analytical person ____
5. **misogyny:** love of women ____
6. **altruist:** selfish person ____
7. **anathema:** object of respect ____
8. **disparage:** praise ____

Check your results: 1-O, 2-O, 3-O, 4-S, 5-O, 6-O, 7-O, 8-O.

Test 3: What's the word?

Write in the appropriate blank the word which most closely fits each definition.

1. An object of hatred _____
2. Tendency to analyze one's thoughts, feelings, motives, etc.
3. To deprive of all force or strength _____
4. One who is interested in others' welfare _____
5. Self-seeking flatterer _____
6. One who has imaginary ailments _____
7. To belittle, express a low estimate of _____
8. Hatred of women _____

Check your results: 1-anathema, 2-introversion, 3-enervate, 4-altruist, 5-sycophant, 6-hypochondriac, 7-disparage, 8-misogyny.

All right. You've seen these eight words. You've thought about them. You've looked them up. You've pronounced them. You've spelled them. You've reacted to them in a variety of different ways. And so now they are yours—no one can ever take them from you.

This has happened in perhaps only thirty minutes.

Is this good? It is absolutely spectacular. The average person who takes no active steps toward improving his vocabulary learns at most twenty-five to fifty new words a year. Yet by following the simple and easy procedures outlined here you can add eight to fifteen new words (to say nothing of the scores of derivative forms) to your vocabulary every day you read—two thousand to three thousand words a year!

ELEVENTH DAY

Is Your Vocabulary Average, Good, Excellent, or Superior?

Four more tests to tell you where you stand.

Everybody realizes the value of a large vocabulary. There is no doubt that the better a person's verbal equipment, the more accurately he can think about and analyze life's complex problems.

Here are four more tests that will give you a reliable comparison of your vocabulary with the average.

Is Your Vocabulary Average?

If it is, you should be able to determine in at least four instances out of five whether word and definition are the *same* (S) or *opposite* (O) in meaning:

1. **audacity:** boldness ____
2. **incessant:** never-ending ____
3. **adept:** awkward ____
4. **to scoff:** to respect
5. **precise:** accurate ____

Check your results: 1-S, 2-S, 3-O, 4-O, 5-S.

Is Your Vocabulary Good?

Then you will be able to check the correct meaning of at least four of the following five words.

1. **mercenary:** (a) influenced exclusively by money; (b) commercial; (c) expensive
2. **arrogant:** (a) shy; (b) excessively proud and self-confident; (c) intelligent, possessed of a keen mind
3. **to replenish:** (a) use carefully; (b) save for future use; (c) renew, refill
4. **gourmand:** (a) ravenous eater, glutton; (b) stickler for etiquette; (l) wealthy man, plutocrat
5. **frugal:** (a) thrifty; (b) extravagant; (c) foolish

Check your results: 1-a, 2-b, 3-c, 4-a, 5-a.

Is Your Vocabulary Excellent?

Then you should be able to match *all* the words in column 1 with their correct synonyms in column 2:

1. **crass**
2. **opulent**
3. **nebulous**
4. **pedantic**
5. **adamant**

(a) wealthy
(b) showing off one's learning
(c) basic
(d) cruel
(e) indistinct
(f) unyielding
(g) crude

Check your results: 1-g, 2-a, 3-e, 4-b, 5-f.

Is Your Vocabulary Superior?

Then you will define these difficult words correctly:
1. **contrite:** (a) remorseful; (b) irritable; (c) trustworthy
2. **vagary:** (a) rare gem; (b) wild idea, freakish whim; (c) pleasant surprise
3. **to obfuscate:** (a) misunderstand; (b) solve; (c) confuse, bewilder
4. **parsimonious:** (a) religious; (b) stingy; (c) hypocritical
5. **anathema:** (a) drug that alleviates pain; (b) philosophy of life; (c) object of deep hatred

Check your results: 1-a, 2-b, 3-c, 4-b, 5-c.

TWELFTH DAY

A New Way to Build Your Vocabulary

Roots provide clues that can help you decipher new words for yourself and increase your vocabulary.

One of the quickest, surest, and most permanent methods of increasing your vocabulary is to study groups of words containing a common root. Learn the root and you'll never forget the word.

The means by which English words are derived from foreign roots is called *etymology*. From now on, we'll constantly be referring to the etymology, or etymological basis or meaning, of the new words we discuss.

Here is an example of how this system works: Latin **pedis** means *foot*, and as an etymological root is spelled **ped-** in such words as **pedestrian** (someone who goes on foot, or, more wryly apropos in this modern age of the automobile, a motorist who has finally found a parking place); **pedal** (a lever controlled by the foot); and **pedestal** (the foot, or base, of a column, statue, etc.). Knowing that the English syllable **ped-** has some relationship to *foot*, you can easily understand, and even more easily remember, the following important words:

Biped: a creature with two feet. Man is a **biped;** birds are also **bipeds.** So the root **bi-** must mean *two*, as also in **bicycle,** a two-wheeled vehicle.

48

Quadruped: a creature with four feet. Dogs, cats, lions, tigers, and most other mammals are **quadrupeds.** So the root **quadr-** must mean *four,* as also in **quadrilateral,** a geometric figure with four sides.

Impede: to hinder the progress of, get in the way of. An **impediment,** then, is a hindrance or obstruction, something that gets in the way of progress. A speech **impediment,** such as a stammer or stutter, gets in the way of fluency—almost as if one spoke with one's foot in one's mouth! Etymologically, an **impediment** tangles up someone's feet so that progress is difficult or impossible.

Expedite: the opposite of **impede,** this verb means to speed or facilitate the progress of—the road was widened to **expedite** traffic. The adjective **expeditious** means rapid, prompt, without delay—for example, the **expeditious** movements of goods and mail by airplane. To **expedite** is, etymologically, to free the feet for easy and rapid progress.

Another Way of Saying foot

Biped, quadruped, impede, and **expedite** are all built on the root **ped-,** from Latin *pedis, foot.* The Greeks too had a word for *foot: podis,* which occurs in English words as the *root* **pod-.** Consider for example:

Podiatrist: one who treats foot ailments, such as corns, calluses, fallen arches, etc.—the specialty is **podiatry.** Here we meet another new root, **iatr-,** meaning *medical treatment.* **Podiatrists** are specialists in the medical treatment of feet, just as **psychiatrists** specialize in the medical treatment of the psyche, or mind.

Chiropodist: an older term for **podiatrist,** the latter being the official designation. Most foot doctors put both titles on their shingles, and the two words have exactly the same

49

meaning. The specialty is **chiropody**. **Chiropodist** combines **pod-**, *foot*, with Greek *chiro-*, *hand:* in earlier days, when people did more manual work, instead of merely pushing buttons, hands as well as feet required medical treatment.

Podium: a raised platform for a speaker or orchestra conductor. Etymologically, a **podium** is a base, or foot, on which to stand.

Tripod: any support with three legs (or, etymologically, feet), as for a camera, telescope, etc. So **tri-** means *three*, as in **triangle** (a figure with three angles), just as **bi-** means *two* and **quadr-** means *four*.

Test Your Learning

Notice how simple it is to understand, and how effectively (and expeditiously!) you can remember the words we have discussed when you see clearly how each one is built on the root **ped-** or **pod-**, when you sense the idea of "footness" in all of them. Now, to make them a useful part of your vocabulary, to really nail them down as permanent acquisitions, try the following exercises.

Say the Words

The first, and the most fruitful, step you can take in adding a word to your vocabulary is to understand, by knowing its root, why it means what it does. The next step is to become used to it, to get on relaxed and friendly terms with it by hearing it in your own voice. So say each word aloud, not once, but several times, following carefully the phonetic respelling. In this way you not only make friends with a new word, but you also feel so at ease with it that it will pop up in your thinking and conversation without any conscious effort on your part.

> The symbol ə indicates the very slight vowel sound heard in the first syllable of *commit* (kə-MIT') or the last syllable of *Linda* (LIN'-də). The accent mark (') shows stress, capitalized syllables receiving a stronger stress than those in lower case.

1. **biped:** BY'-ped
2. **quadruped:** KWAHD'-roo-ped
3. **impede:** im-PEED'
4. **impediment:** im-PED'-ə-mənt
5. **expedite:** EKS'-pə-dite
6. **expeditious:** eks'-pə-DISH'-əs
7. **podiatrist:** pə-DY'-ə-trist
8. **chiropodist:** kə-ROP'-ə-dist
9. **podium:** PO'-dee-əm
10. **tripod:** TRY'-pod

Think with the Words

You understand these words, you're comfortable saying them, so now you're ready to start thinking with them. (And bear in mind that every word you learn, or become more thoroughly acquainted with, is an added tool for thinking.)

Pair up the definitions in column 1 below with the words in column 2, writing your answers in the space provided:

1. official designation for foot doctor ____   (a) **biped**
2. older term for a foot doctor ____   (b) **quadruped**
3. two-footed creature ____   (c) **impede**
4. speaker's stand ____   (d) **impediment**
5. four-footed creature ____   (f) **expeditious**
6. to make easier or quicker ____   (e) **expedite**
7. three-legged stand ____   (g) **podiatrist**
8. to get in the way of ____   (h) **chiropodist**
9. without delay ____   (i) **podium**
10. obstruction ____   (j) **tripod**

Check your results: 1-g, 2-h, 3-a, 4-i, 5-b, 6-e, 7-j, 8-c, 9-f, 10-d.

Use the Words

You understand the words, you've said them, you've thought about them: now can you use them when you need them? In the following sentences, supply the word that meaningfully completes each thought:

1. A camera is often mounted on a _____.
2. Unlike most other mammals, man is a _____.
3. Unlike man, a wolf, cow, or horse is a _____.
4. A foot doctor is called either a _____ or a _____.
5. Narrow roads and frequent stoplights _____ the rapid flow of traffic.
6. Most states are building wide, limited-access highways to _____ traffic.
7. Military roads accommodate the _____ movement of troops and vehicles.
8. A speaker delivers his address from a _____.
9. His unpleasant personality is an _____ to his advancement in the company.

Check your results: 1-tripod; 2-biped; 3-quadruped; 4-chiropodist, podiatrist; 5-impede; 6-expedite; 7-expeditious; 8-podium; 9-impediment.

Remember the Roots

The roots you have learned have brought you to a quick understanding of ten valuable words. As you will realize shortly, these same roots can unlock for you the meaning of scores of additional new words you may meet in your reading or hear in conversation. So, are you sure you have them straight? Match the following columns.

1. ped- ____   (a) three
2. bi- ____   (b) two
3. quadr- ____   (c) foot
4. pod- ____   (d) medical treatment
5. iatr- ____   (e) hand
6. psych- ____   (f) four
7. chiro- ____   (g) mind
8. tri- ____

Check your results: 1-c, 2-b, 3-f, 4-c, 5-d, 6-g, 7-e, 8-a.

Another Kind of ped-

There is no more effective means of learning new words quickly, permanently, and in wholesale quantities than by seeing how they occur in etymological families. By examining the **ped-** and **pod-** families, you have, in a few minutes, made a strong and lasting contact with ten valuable words, and in addition have learned *six* useful new roots. Now let us look at another **ped-** family, one that comes to us, not from Latin *pedis* or Greek *podis,* but from Greek *paidos.*

The Greek word *paidos* means *child*. In English terms built on *paidos,* the root is again spelled **ped-**, although it has no relation, despite its identical appearance, to Latin **ped-**, *foot*. For example:

pediatrics: the medical specialty of children's diseases. The doctor is a **pediatrician.** Once again our friend **iatr-**, *medical treatment.*

pedagogy: The science, art, or principles of teaching. This word combines **paidos,** *child*, with the Greek **agogos,** *to lead.* Hence, etymologically, **pedagogy** is the leading of children.

pedagogue: a teacher—usually one who is stuffy, excessively precise, or dogmatic. The word is not a bit complimentary, and indicates our irritation with teachers who flaunt their learning and make it a practice to correct our errors.

orthopedics: the medical specialty dealing with bones and joints. Broken legs, curvature of the spine, club foot, and other skeletal injuries or deformities are the province of the **orthopedist** or **orthopedic surgeon**. This word combines **paidos,** *child,* and the root **ortho-,** *straight* or *correct*—the idea being that a child's bones are more pliable and hence more easily straightened, corrected, or mended than those of an adult. Of course, an **orthopedist** does not by any means limit his practice to children.

New Roots Lead to New Words

Building your vocabulary through an exploration of etymological roots is not only amazingly simple, rapid, and effective, but also remarkably productive. An excursion into one family of words automatically turns up new families that promise endless and exciting discoveries—as you have already seen. Starting with Latin *pedis,* you were soon involved with Greek *podis* and *paidos.* You learned, or became reacquainted with, a score of vital, useful words, and discovered new roots that unlocked still more new words.

Suppose, therefore, we continue the process of letting roots lead to new words, which in turn lead to new roots, which in turn . . . etc., by looking again at **bi-,** meaning *two.*

bigamy: etymologically, two marriages. The **bigamist** takes a second wife or husband (statistically, far fewer women than men commit bigamy) while a previous union is still in effect. The adjective is **bigamous.** So **gam-** must mean *marriage.* Let us see what interesting words this new root leads us to.

monogamy: the system of only one marriage at a time. The adjective is **monogamous.** So **mon-** must mean *one,* as in **monocle,** a lens for one eye, and **monarch,** the one supreme ruler of a nation. Knowing the meaning of **mon-,** can you figure out **monologue, monoplane, monosyllable?**

polygamy: the custom in which a man has many wives (or

marriages), once practiced by the Mormons in Utah. The adjective is **polygamous**. So **poly-** must mean *many*, as in **polygon**, a geometric figure of many sides. Can you then figure out **polysyllable**, **polyglot** (**glot-** means *tongue* or *language*), **polytheism** (*theos* means *god*)?

misogamy: the hatred of marriage. The adjective is **misogamous**, the hater is a **misogamist**. So **mis-** (from Greek *misein*) must mean *hatred*.

misanthropy: the hatred of all mankind. The person who hates everyone is a **misanthrope**. The adjective is **misanthropic**. So **anthrop-** must mean *mankind*, as in **anthropology**, the science of mankind's development, and **philanthropy**, the love of mankind (**phil-** means *love*).

misogyny: the hatred of women. A **misogynist** hates all females, usually for dark reasons that only a psychiatrist can unravel. The adjective is **misogynous**. So **gyn-** must mean *woman*, as in **gynecology**, the medical study of ailments peculiar to women.

Let us pause in our etymological excursions at this point and consolidate our recent discoveries.

Test Your Learning

Say the Words

Pronounce each word aloud several times:

1. **pediatrics**: pee-dee-AT'-riks
2. **pedagogy**: PED'-ə-gō-jee
3. **pedagogue**: PED'-ə-gog
4. **orthopedics**: awr'-thə-PEE'-diks
5. **bigamy**: BIG'-ə-mee
6. **monogamy**: mə-NOG'-ə-mee
7. **polygamy**: pə-LIG'-ə-mee
8. **misogamy**: mə-SOG'-ə-mee
9. **misanthropy**: mə-SAN'-thrə-pee
10. **misogyny**: mə-SOJ'-ə-nee

Think with the Words

Match the columns:

1. hatred of women ____
2. one marriage at a time ____
3. a "schoolmarmish" teacher ____
4. specialty of children's diseases ____
5. plurality of wives ____
6. art of teaching ____
7. crime of additional marriage without divorce, annulment, etc. ____
8. hatred of all mankind ____
9. medical treatment of skeletal injuries or deformities ____
10. hatred of marriage ____

(a) **pediatrics**
(b) **pedagogy**
(c) **pedagogue**
(d) **orthopedics**
(e) **bigamy**
(f) **monogamy**
(g) **polygamy**
(h) **misogamy**
(i) **misanthropy**
(j) **misogyny**

Check your results: 1-j, 2-f, 3-c, 4-a, 5-g, 6-b, 7-e, 8-i, 9-d, 10-h.

Use the Words

Fill in the blanks to make meaningful sentences. Forms of the words other than those in the pronunciation list may sometimes be required, such as **pediatrician, orthopedist,** etc.

1. A _____ shuns females—love for them is beyond his capacity.
2. The specialist who sets bone fractures is known as an _____.
3. Mothers take their infants to a _____ for a medical checkup.
4. One husband, one wife: this is the system known as _____.
5. A sailor with a wife in every port is a _____.
6. Those who are preparing to teach take college courses in _____.
7. The hatred of a _____ is directed against the entire human race.
8. _____ is no longer sanctioned in this country, but at one time was practiced by the Mormons.

9. There are those who direct their hatred against institutions instead of people. A _____, for example, hates marriage.

10. A stuffy, straitlaced teacher is referred to, derogatively, as a _____.

Check your results: 1-misogynist; 2-orthopedist, orthopedic surgeon; 3-pediatrician; 4-monogamy; 5-bigamist; 6-pedogogy; 7-misanthrope; 8-polygamy; 9-misogamist; 10-pedagogue.

Remember the Roots

Match roots and meanings:

1. paidos ____   (a) one
2. agogos ____   (b) god
3. ortho- ____   (c) mankind
4. gam- ____   (d) woman
5. mon- ____   (e) love
6. poly- ____   (f) child
7. mis- ____   (g) marriage
8. anthrop- ____   (h) tongue, language
9. phil- ____   (i) straight, correct
10. gyn- ____   (j) to lead
11. glot- ____   (k) hatred
12. theos- ____   (l) many

Check your results: 1-f, 2-j, 3-i, 4-g, 5-a, 6-l, 7-k, 8-c, 9-e, 10-d, 11-h, 12-b.

A Few Roots Unlock the Secrets of Hundreds of Words

So far we have made contact with twenty extremely productive Latin and Greek roots, and intensively studied twenty English words plus their derivative forms. In our quick excursions into roots, however, we noticed in passing another twenty or so words—many of them perhaps quite new to you. And yet we have hardly begun to tap the rich resources of the roots we've uncovered.

You can take the most complex words—any number of them—and if you can recognize the roots on which they're built you will have no difficulty understanding them, remembering them, and keeping them unconfused in your mind. By becoming familiar with the common roots we've discussed, you have taken a giant step forward in building a larger and more meaningful vocabulary, for you are now able to figure out hundreds of words that you may never have seen or heard before.

So at this point let us go back into etymology. We'll take another quick look at some of the roots we've been working with, and see how easy it is to discover twenty-seven additional words, even though we'll hardly do much more than scratch the surface.

Doesn't recognizing the root of the following words make them immediately understandable and almost absurdly simple to remember?

ped-, *foot:*
   centipede, a wormlike creature that seems to have a hundred feet—of course an exaggeration
   velocipede, a child's tricycle propelled by speedy feet

bi-, *two:*
   bisect, to cut into two equal parts
   bilingual, able to speak two languages
   biennial, every two years
   bilateral, having, or involving, two sides

tri-, *three:*
   triplets, three children at a single birth
   trisect, to cut into three equal parts
   trilingual, able to speak three languages
   triennial, every three years

quadr-, *four:*
  quadruplets, four children at a single birth
  quadrennial, every four years
  quadrisyllable, a word of four syllables

ortho-, *straight, correct:*
  orthodontia, the branch of dentistry dealing with straightening the teeth, correcting the bite, etc.
  orthography, correct writing, hence the system of spelling a language

agogos, *to lead:*
  demagogue, one who pretends to be a leader of the people, but in actuality foments discontent among the masses in order to gain power
  synagogue, Jewish temple in which people are led or brought together to worship God

anthrop-, *mankind:*
  anthropoid, similar to man in form or appearance, as the anthropoid apes

theos, *god:*
  theology, the study of God or religion
  monotheism, belief in one God
  atheism, complete disbelief in the existence of God

phil-, *love:*
  Philadelphia, the city of brotherly love
  philology, the love of words—hence the science of language
  philter, a love potion
  philander, to make love triflingly and insincerely
  bibliophile, one who loves books; also a collector of books
  philatelist, a stamp collector; etymologically, one who loves stamps

Let's Tie It All Up

In the short time it took you to cover the material in this day's material, you have either learned for the first time, or become reaquainted with on a deeper level, approximately sixty-seven expressive and highly useful English words—more than the average person learns in two years. More important, you have come to realize that words, like people, grow in families, and that the parent in these families is often a Greek or Latin root.

When you have control of a root, you are in command of scores of words; you can figure out the meaning of words you may never have seen before; you understand words more fully; you know why a word means what it does.

And from now on you will probably note a curious phenomenon. The words you have studied today will begin to appear over and over again in your reading—not because they have suddenly become popular, but because you have a mind-set toward them that will make them doubly conspicuous, and considerably more meaningful, every time you meet them.

Very soon—and this you will shortly discover for yourself—you will begin to use these new words without hesitation or self-consciousness.

So now, to wrap it all in a neat little package, are you ready to try a simple test on etymology? Here are twenty words chosen at random from the sixty-seven we've worked with. In each, a single root is printed in boldface type. Can you write the English meaning of each such root in the blank provided:

1. **exped**itious   _____
2. **ped**agogy   _____
3. **mono**gamy   _____
4. **poly**glot   _____
5. **mis**ogyny   _____
6. **ped**iatrics   _____
7. **pod**iatry   _____
8. **bi**lingual   _____

9. **triennial** _____
10. **chiropodist** _____
11. **demagogue** _____
12. **misanthropy** _____
13. **polytheism** _____
14. **philanthropy** _____
15. **orthopedics** _____
16. **theology** _____
17. **quadruped** _____
18. **psychiatry** _____
19. **polygamy** _____
20. **gynecology** _____

Check your results: 1-foot; 2-child; 3-one; 4-tongue, language; 5-hatred; 6-medical treatment; 7-foot; 8-two; 9-three; 10-hand; 11-to lead; 12-mankind; 13-many; 14-love; 15-straight, correct; 16-god; 17-four; 18-mind; 19-marriage; 20-woman.

THIRTEENTH DAY

Let's Learn Ten New Words

A quick warmup that will help you add some short and expressive terms to your vocabulary.

Do you have a good stock of short, graphic terms with which to express your ideas? Complete as many of the following words as you can; then add to your vocabulary by studying the key that follows the test:

1. dark, grayish-blue in color — l_____id
2. heated or vehement in spirit — f_____id
3. extreme in opinion or practice — r_____id
4. wan, without color — p_____id
5. clear, easily understood — l_____id
6. diseased, gruesome, easily influenced by ideas of a gloomy nature — m_____id
7. filthy, dirty, mean — s_____id
8. frank, honest, truthful — c_____id
9. bright, sharp, clear — v_____id
10. glaringly sensational, marked by violent passion or crime — l_____id

1. **Livid.** This can best be understood by thinking of a black-and-blue bruise. Also used figuratively, as **livid** with rage, when the face takes on this unpleasant color.

2. **Fervid.** A **fervid** attitude is ardent and zealous; a **fervid** attack is warm and passionate. This word comes from a Latin verb meaning *to boil* or *flame*.

3. **Rabid.** A **rabid** person is fanatical, goes to extreme lengths in expressing an opinion or taking a stand. This word is from a Latin stem meaning *to rave,* the same stem from which we derive **rabies,** the disease that affects dogs.

4. **Pallid.** This word is essentially similar in meaning to pale, except for its added implication that color or health has been lost through some abnormal condition such as weakness, illness, fainting, fatigue, etc.

5. **Lucid.** If anything is **lucid,** it is clear or easy to understand. We may speak of **lucid** prose, a **lucid** argument, or of a mental patient whose mind is no longer **lucid.**

6. **Morbid.** In its medical sense, **morbid** implies lack of health, as in a **morbid** condition of the lungs or a **morbid** growth on the intestines; in its extended and more general meaning, the word implies unnatural gruesomeness or gloomy pessimism, as in the **morbid** cartoons of Charles Addams or the **morbid** atmosphere of Russian novels. The word derives from the Latin *morbus, disease.*

7. **Sordid.** This is a difficult word to explain because so much of its impact comes from its emotional flavor rather than from its direct meaning. A **sordid** atmosphere implies repulsiveness and degradation, lack of cleanliness and cheerfulness, perhaps even an open display of base passions or immorality. **Sordid** surroundings might be mean, dirty, indicative of dire poverty. A **sordid** book might deal with vile people and foul doings. The word comes from the Latin *sordere, to be dirty.*

8. **Candid.** A **candid** person is frank, aboveboard, not given to deception or concealment. If you are noted for your **candidness,** you do not attempt to hide what you know, even at the risk of hurting people's feelings or putting yourself at a disadvantage. The word is from the Latin *toga candida,* the white (for purity) garment worn by Roman office seekers,

who thereby signified that they had nothing to conceal; and it is from the same root that we get the word **candidate.**

9. **Vivid.** A **vivid** picture is sharp and clear; **vivid** colors are brilliant, like bright red or green, rather than dull, like gray or black; a **vivid** account appeals powerfully to the imagination, has a sharp impact on the emotions, etc. The word is from the Latin *vivere, to be alive.*

10. **Lurid.** A woman with a **lurid** past has lived sensationally, notoriously, scandalously; the **lurid** details of death, catastrophe, etc., are those which might offend the sensitive reader or listener; such extreme details might be excessively gruesome, repugnant, or disgusting.

FOURTEENTH DAY

A Challenge to Your Vocabulary

Here are fifty more words that should be in every educated person's vocabulary. How successfully can you learn them?

A test can be used for one of two purposes: to check on your knowledge, or to motivate your learning. These tests have the latter end in view.

It is true in a sense that if you cannot answer a question you thereby display your ignorance. It is equally true, and far more important, that when you finally discover the correct answer you thereupon erase that ignorance.

In the five tests which follow, you will be asked fifty questions, and your learning will come from the questions you *cannot answer*. Each test will take you no more than three minutes. Go through them quickly, guessing as wildly as you like; then pay particular attention to the answers. For every mistake you make, you will learn a new word. The more errors, the more words you will add to your vocabulary. So have no fear of coming through with a low score; the lower it is, the greater your gain!

Test 1: People

1. Babies are delivered by (a) a **pediatrician**; (b) an **osteopath**; (c) an **obstetrician**.
2. Teeth are straightened by (a) an **orthodontist**; (b) a **podiatrist**; (c) an **orthopedist**.

3. Music is played superbly by (a) a **chanteuse**; (b) a **tyro**; (c) a **virtuoso**.

4. A loudmouthed, turbulent woman is (a) a **feminist**; (b) a **virago**; (c) an **executrix**.

5. A politician who tries to cause unrest among the masses so that he may gain his own selfish ends is (a) a **reactionary**; (b) a **demagogue**; (c) a **radical**.

6. Someone who arranges a ballet is (a) a **choreographer**; (b) a **thespian**; (c) a **terpsichorean**.

7. A doctor who performs eye surgery is (a) an **ophthalmologist**; (b) an **optician**; (c) an **optometrist**.

8. Someone who dabbles in the arts is (a) a **gourmet**; (b) a **connoisseur**; (c) a **dilettante**.

9. Someone who has dedicated his life to beauty is (a) a **voluptuary**; (b) an **esthete**; (c) an **ascetic**.

10. A stamp collector is (a) a **bibliophile**; (b) a **numismatist**; (c) a **philatelist**.

Check your results: 1-c, 2-a, 3-c, 4-b, 5-b, 6-a, 7-a, 8-c, 9-b, 10-c.

Test 2: Sciences

1. **Anthropology** deals with the development of (a) plants; (b) animals; (c) mankind.

2. **Astronomy** is concerned with (a) rocks; (b) stars; (c) insects.

3. **Semantics** explores (a) the meanings of words; (b) the source of words; (c) the use of words.

4. **Entomology** deals with (a) words; (b) insects; (c) fish.

5. **Etymology** deals with (a) words; (b) insects; (c) fish.

6. **Eugenics** is the science of (a) social conditions; (b) better offspring; (c) atomic energy.

7. **Dermatology** relates to diseases of the (a) digestive tract; (b) skin; (c) feet.

8. **Ornithology** is concerned with (a) birds; (b) reptiles; (c) climate.

9. **Geriatrics** attempts to solve the problems of (a) infancy; (b) adolescence; (c) old age.

10. **Genetics** is interested in (a) herdity; (b) conservation; (c) mineral resources.

Check your results: 1-c, 2-b, 3-a, 4-b, 5-a, 6-b, 7-b, 8-a, 9-c, 10-a.

Test 3: Abnormal States

Answer *yes* (Y) or *no* (N):

1. **Amnesia** means loss of memory. ____
2. **Aphasia** affects the ability to walk. ____
3. A **somnambulist** walks in his sleep. ____
4. **Insomnia** keeps one up at night. ____
5. A **neurosis** is more serious than a **psychosis**. ____
6. **Claustrophobia** is fear of open spaces. ____
7. **Dipsomania** is related to thievery. ____
8. **Acrophobia** is fear of high places. ____
9. **Egocentricity** is a morbid interest in oneself. ____
10. **Pyromania** is related to fire. ____

Check your results: 1-Y; 2-N (**aphasia** is loss or impairment of the ability to use language); 3-Y; 4-Y; 5-N (a **neurosis** is an emotional disorder caused by conflicts, tensions, insecurity, etc.—a **psychosis** is a severe form of mental derangement); 6-N (**claustrophobia** is morbid fear of enclosed spaces—**agoraphobia** is fear of open places); 7-N (**dipsomania** is another name for alcoholism—**kleptomania** is related to thievery); 8-Y; 9-Y; 10-Y (the **pyromaniac** has a morbid and irresistible compulsion to set fires).

Test 4: Actions

Are the meanings given for the following words *true* (T) or *false* (F)?

1. **verify**: to ascertain the truth of something. ____
2. **soliloquize**: to think silently about something. ____
3. **alleviate**: to aggravate the pain of something. ____
4. **deprecate**: to belittle. ____
5. **cower**: to stand up bravely to danger. ____

6. **cavil:** to raise trivial objections. ____
7. **badger:** to torment, annoy, harass. ____
8. **temporize:** to meet one's obligations promptly. ____
9. **meander:** to wander aimlessly ____
10. **malign:** to recommend someone heartily ____

Check your results: 1-T; 2-F (**soliloquize** means to talk aloud to oneself); 3-F (**alleviate** means to diminish the pain); 4-T; 5-F (to **cower** is to crouch in fear); 6-T; 7-T; 8-F (if you **temporize**, you play for time, postpone, or procrastinate); 9-T; 10-F (to **malign** someone is to slander him).

Test 5: Comparisons

Indicate whether the following paired words mean the *same* (S) or *opposite* (O):

1. parsimonious: prodigal ____
2. aquiline: straight ____
3. taciturn: loquacious ____
4. exigency: emergency ____
5. enervated: exhausted ____
6. erudite: ignorant ____
7. apathetic: lethargic ____
8. savor: flavor ____
9. inclement: mild ____
10. coquetry: flirtatiousness ____

Check your results: 1-O (**parsimonious** is stingy—**prodigal** is extravagant); 2-O (**aquiline** means beaked, curved); 3-O (**taciturn** means quiet, disinclined to talk—**loquacious** means talkative); 4-S; 5-S, 6-O (**erudite** means learned); 7-S (both words mean having or exhibiting little or no feeling); 8-S; 9-O (**inclement** means harsh, unfavorable); 10-S.

Test Your Learning

Now, to show you how easy it is to add to your vocabulary, let me offer you a quick test designed to check your learning.

Spend a little time examining your mistakes, if any, and let the correct answers erase such areas of ignorance as the original test may have revealed. Then, when you are ready, take this last test.

Directions. Write one of the words discussed in these pages which best fits the brief definition. The initial letter is offered to guide your thinking:

1. first assistant to the stork: o_____
2. accomplished musician: v_____
3. arranger of the ballet: c_____
4. devotee of beauty: e_____
5. science of heavenly bodies: a_____
6. study of insects: e_____
7. study of heredity: g_____
8. science that deals with the problems of old age: g_____
9. loss of memory: a_____
10. loss of power to use language: a_____
11. alcoholism: d_____
12. fear of restricted areas: c_____
13. to speak aloud to oneself: s_____
14. to lessen pain: a_____
15. to crouch in fear: c_____
16. to slander or gossip about someone: m_____
17. tightfisted: p_____
18. worn out with fatigue: e_____
19. harsh, unfavorable: i_____
20. learned, versed in book knowledge: e_____

Check your results: 1-obstetrician; 2-virtuoso; 3-choreographer; 4-esthete; 5-astronomy; 6-entomology; 7-genetics; 8-geriatrics; 9-amnesia; 10-aphasia; 11-dipsomania; 12-claustrophobia; 13-soliloquize; 14-alleviate; 15-cower; 16-malign; 17-parsimonious; 18-**enervated;** 19-inclement; 20-erudite.

FIFTEENTH DAY

Just for Fun

A Speller's Lament

There are only twenty-six letters in the alphabet. So why all the confusion and disorder?

If a spirit is a **ghost,** why is someone to whom we extend hospitality not a **ghest?** And if **palm** is the way we have to spell it, why isn't one of our fingers a **thulm?**

All right, so there's a **b** in **plumber.** Then why can't we drive nails with a **hamber?**

And if we sing a **hymn,** why don't we **dymn** the lights?

What a language! How's an unsuspecting soul to know that there's an **s** in **viscount?** Or an **l** in **solder?** Or a **c** in **victuals?**

If we say **kee,** why do we write it **quay?**

And when are they going to get around to spelling **colonel** so that it looks like what it is?

Perhaps someone can explain why it's O.K. to spell it either **marvelous** or **marvellous,** but scandalous to spell it **scandallous.** Or why, if **whiskey** can also be **whisky, monkey** can't be **monky.**

Why, if almost everybody wants to spell it **ukelele,** does the dictionary insist on **ukulele?**

Doesn't the rule plainly say that **i** comes before **e,** except after **c?** Then how come **leisure, weird,** and **seize?**

Hoald me back befoar I commicht mayhemb on the neerest dicsionery!

The Misplaced Months

If you have ever studied Latin, you have no doubt wondered why **September,** named after the Latin numeral *septem* (*seven*), stands for our ninth month. And why October, November, and December, respectively from the Roman numbers *octo* (*eight*), *novem* (*nine*), and *decem* (*ten*), actually refer to our tenth, eleventh, and twelfth months. The explanation is simple: the old Roman calendar started with March, not January; and September, October, November, and December *were* the seventh, eighth, ninth, and tenth months in primitive Roman times. When we revised the calendar, we slipped in two extra months at the beginning of the year, but never changed the four misleading names.

What's Wrong With This?

1. *This criteria is not, in my opinion, very reliable.*

Criteria is a plural noun, although admittedly it has an amazing resemblance to a singular. (The singular form is **criterion.**) Hence, adjective **this** and verb **is** should also be plural. Correct form: *These criteria are not ... reliable.*

2. *The alumni of Girls High School will hold their annual meeting in April.*

Graduates of a girls' school would likely be females. **Alumni** (pronounced a-LUM'-nye), plural of **alumnus,** refers only to males. Correct form here: **alumnae** (pronounced a-LUM'-nee), plural of **alumna,** feminine form of **alumnus.**

3. *Why don't you lay down for a nap before dinner?*

The verb is wrong. **Lay** means *to place* or *put.* The required form, which would mean *to rest* or *recline,* is **lie.**

4. *I'm surprised I didn't get an invite to his party.*

Invite may be used only as a verb. Proper form: **invitation.**

5. *What an aggravating child she is!*

The original meaning of **aggravate** was *to make worse, to intensify,* and so grammarians have in the past warned against its use as a synonym for **exasperate** or **irritate**. However, words change with usage, and since **aggravating** is now widely used, in both speech and writing, with the meaning of **annoying,** the sentence as it stands is acceptable English.

6. *No one but I can help you.*

In this sentence, **but** means **except,** and is a preposition. According to grammatical rule, prepositions govern the objective case of the pronoun; hence the proper phrasing would be: *No one but me can help you.*

7. *It is I who is responsible for this trouble.*

Who takes the same verb as its antecedent would. The antecedent of **who** here is **I.** Since we say **I am,** not **I is,** the sentence should read: *It is I who am responsible.* . . .

8. *Can I borrow your pen if you're not using it?*

Purists rail against the use of **can** to seek permission, and parents from time immemorial (and with little success) have attempted to train their children to show politeness by using **may** as a substitute. Nevertheless, it is today established and cultivated usage to ask permission with **can.**

9. *What effect does he have on you?*

Except with a special and technical meaning in psychology, **affect** is used only as a verb. Here a noun is required. Correct form: **effect.**

10. *How does he effect you?*

In this sentence, a verb is required. Correct form: **affect.**

PART IV

Spell It Right

In just five days, you can improve your spelling skill almost miraculously.

SIXTEENTH DAY

Special Tricks That Will Make You a Better Speller

> *Learning to be a good speller may seem difficult, but there are tested short cuts to quick and permanent mastery of the words most people misspell.*

Everyone Has Trouble with Spelling

English spelling is without a doubt the most perplexing, the most confounding, the most contradictory, and the most frustrating system of combining letters ever devised by man.

No wonder, therefore, that few people feel any security or self-confidence about their ability to spell correctly, or that only the rare person is always sure whether or not to double a consonant (**embarassment** or **embarrassment, cooly** or **coolly?**); whether to write **ie** or **ei** (**wierd** or **weird, niece** or **neice?**); whether to use **-able** or **-ible** (**irresistable** or **irresistible, indispensable** or **indispensible?**) or whether to end a word with **-ance** or **-ence** (**perseverance** or **perseverence, insistance** or **insistence?**).

Nor should it be a surprise that even people who are completely literate in every other way have trouble with spelling. Novelist F. Scott Fitzgerald was a notoriously bad speller. So was Andrew Jackson, who, when he was twitted on his frequent errors, retorted characteristically, "Well, sir, it's a poor mind that cannot think of more than one way to spell a word!"

And yet, despite the problems caused by our out-of-date,

inconsistent, and complicated spelling system, the average person is a better speller than he may realize—for 95 per cent of his errors occur in a list of about 100 fairly common words that he may use over and over again in his writing. These are demons that seem to have, as it were, two spellings: a correct form and a popular, frequently used, but totally incorrect and unacceptable, form. And both patterns usually look equally good to the untrained speller.

Let us put it to a test whether you have the same trouble with these words that almost everyone else has.

Below you will find twenty of the top demons on the list, each spelled in two ways: the approved form, and the common misspelling. It is up to you to decide which is correct, *a* or *b*. Consider yourself far above average if you make nine to thirteen proper choices, and a really superior speller if you score fourteen or higher:

1. (a) alright; (b) all right _____
2. (a) supersede; (b) supercede _____
3. (a) embarassed; (b) embarrassed _____
4. (a) drunkeness; (b) drunkenness _____
5. (a) irresistible; (b) irresistable _____
6. (a) occurrance; (b) occurrence _____
7. (a) ecstasy; (b) ecstacy _____
8. (a) anoint; (b) annoint _____
9. (a) occassion; (b) occasion _____
10. (a) disappoint; (b) dissapoint _____
11. (a) analize; (b) analyze _____
12. (a) tyranny; (b) tyrrany _____
13. (a) inoculate; (b) inocculate _____
14. (a) cooly; (b) coolly _____
15. (a) indispensable; (b) indispensible _____
16. (a) superintendent; (b) superintendant _____
17. (a) battalion; (b) batallion _____
18. (a) perseverance; (b) perseverence _____
19. (a) iridescent; (b) irridescent _____
20. (a) reccomend; (b) recommend _____

Check your results: 1-b, 2-a, 3-b, 4-b, 5-a, 6-b, 7-a, 8-a, 9-b, 10-a, 11-b, 12-a, 13-a, 14-b, 15-a, 16-a, 17-a, 18-a, 19-a, 20-b.

How to Eliminate Your Trouble

As you discovered from the test you have just taken—or as perhaps you knew all along—English spelling is indeed contradictory and confusing. For example, we must spell it: pro**ceed**, but pre**cede**; **seize**, but **sieze**; resist**ance**, but persist**ence**; indispens**able**, but irresist**ible**; dum**b**, but preferably dumfounded; li**quid**, but li**que**fy; moral**ize**, but anal**yze**; dissi**pate**, but disa**ppoint**; a**nn**ounce, but a**n**oint; a**l**ready, but a**ll** right; preference, but occurrence.

So if you have a sense of inadequacy about your spelling, or if you are confused more often than you are sure, take heart. Investigations have proved that most people not only misspell the same words, but they misspell them in exactly the same way.

It is this fact that makes it so easy for you to achieve a spectacular improvement in your spelling, as well as a considerable increase in your confidence, by spending just a few days in simple self-training. For if you fancy yourself an imperfect or even an extremely poor speller, the chances are that you have developed an inferiority complex solely because you are in doubt about most or all of the approximately one hundred demons with which Part IV of this book deals. Conquer this single list of commonly misspelled words, and in all likelihood 95 per cent of your difficulties will vanish.

How do you go about it?

1. By learning to use a few simple memory-association tricks that will help you choose correct patterns, discard incorrect ones. (Such memory tricks are known technically as *mnemonics,* pronounced ne-MON-iks.)

2. By training both your *visual* memory (so that only the

correct form will *look* proper) and your *muscular* memory (so that you will without a moment's thought or hesitation *write* only the correct forms).

3. By thoroughly understanding how to apply half a dozen clear-cut and serviceable spelling principles that will rule out the slightest possibility of error in certain confusing groups of words.

That doesn't sound very hard, does it? Then let's begin.

Speed!

Eleven—and only eleven—words in our language containing more than one syllable terminate with the sound **seed**. Of these eleven, one ends in **-sede**, three in **-ceed**, and the rest in **-cede**.

It may seem confusing, but it needn't be. In a minute or less you can get these eleven demons permanently straightened out in your mind.

Consider: The only English word that ends in **-sede** is **supersede**.

The only three words that end in **-ceed** are **succeed, proceed,** and **exceed**. All of the other words end in **-cede**.

Now let us use a couple of mnemonics: For **supersede**, think of **Super Suds**, a household soap powder. For **suceed, proceed,** and **exceed**, remember this slogan: The driver who **succeeds** in living longer is the one who **proceeds** with caution and never **exceeds** the **speed** limit. Like **speed**, these three words end in **-eed**.

Let's go over that again: *Super* Suds—*super*sede; *speed*—suc*ceed*, pro*ceed*, ex*ceed*.

Now begin training your visual and muscular memory. Look at each word below for a few seconds; then cover it with your hand or a slip of paper and write it correctly in the blank to its right.

supers**ede** _____
succ**eed** _____
proc**eed** _____
exc**eed** _____

More training: Write the word or words that each mnemonic brings to mind:

Super Suds: _____
Speed: (1) _____
         (2) _____
         (3) _____

And that's all there is to it. Except for one little contradiction (and contradictions are the most normal thing in English spelling): although the **c** of **proceed** is followed by two **e**'s, the noun and adjective forms have only one **e** after the **c**: proc**e**dure, proc**e**dural.

What about the other seven words? These need not be memorized, for you know that every word except **supersede, succeed, proceed,** and **exceed** ends in -**cede**. In case you are curious, however, these seven are: ac**cede**, ante**cede**, con**cede**, inter**cede**, pre**cede**, re**cede**, and se**cede**.

Two Other Confusing Endings

It is insist**ent** or insist**ant**? Persist**ent** or persist**ant**? Depend**ent** or depend**ant**? And how about occur**rence** or occur**rance**, persever**ence** or persever**ance**, abhor**rence** or abhor**rance**? These are confusing, pestiferous questions; yet you may have to come up with the correct answers a score of times in a busy week of writing or typing.

There are hundreds of common words ending in the alternative possibilities we are discussing, but only a relative few are frequently, almost universally, misspelled. These are the words we shall concentrate on. Let us conquer some of these demons by means of mnemonics.

Consider, first, the **superintend*ent*** of an **apartm*ent*** house. What does he come around to collect at the beginning of every month? The **rent,** of course, and is he **insist*ent*** and **persist*ent*** in his collections? He is—because his job is **depend*ent*** on **rent** payments. Notice, then, that the single mnemonic **rent** (which ends in *-ent*) controls four of the top demons in our language: **superintend*ent*, insist*ent*, persist*ent*,** and **depend*ent*.**

Train your visual and muscular responses to these adjectives and to the nouns derived from them. Look at each word, then conceal it with your hand or a card and write it correctly.

superintend*ent*
insist*ent*
persist*ent*
depend*ent*
superintend*ence*
insist*ence*
persist*ence*
depend*ence*

Now consider eleven verbs that end in the letter **r**: **in-FER, pre-FER, re-FER, con-FER, de-FER, oc-CUR, in-CUR, con-CUR, re-CUR, de-TER, ab-HOR.**

You realize that each verb is accented on the last syllable. You will notice also that in each instance the **r** is preceded by a *single* vowel. Now here is one of the very, very few rules of English spelling to which there is no exception: Every verb ending in **r** preceded by a single vowel and accented on the final syllable forms its noun with **-ence.** (Take a few seconds to memorize this principle; you will often find it a lifesaver.)

But wait! Do we double the **r** before adding **-ence,** or do we leave it alone?

We do both (nothing about spelling is easy, as you know), depending on whether the accent stays on the same syllable when the noun is formed or whether it shifts back to the first syllable.

Look at the last six verbs on the list. In each case, the accent remains on the same syllable when we add **-ence: oc-CUR** and **oc-CUR-rence, in-CUR** and **in-CUR-rence,** etc. When the accent stays put, we double the **r**.

Practice on these:

occurrence _____
incurrence _____
concurrence _____
recurrence _____
deterrence _____
abhorrence _____

Now, on the other hand, see what happens with the first five verbs. In each of these, the accent shifts back to the first syllable when you add **-ence: in-FER,** but **IN-fer-ence; pre-FER,** but **PREF-er-ence:** etc. When the accent shifts back, we *do not* double the **r**.

Practice as before:

preference _____
inference _____
reference _____
conference _____
deference _____

We have covered all except one of the words in this category that are most subject to error. This one, which for some unknown reason looks more appealing to the untrained speller when it ends in **-ence,** is correct only with the **-ance** ending: **perseverance.**

Have you got it all straight now? Study this section once again, paying particular attention to the rules and the mnemonics; then ask someone to dictate the words to you in random order. If your learning has been successful, you should make a perfect score on demons that almost everyone else finds troublesome.

SEVENTEENTH DAY

More Memory Tricks to Make You a Perfect Speller

By now you should be convinced that mnemonics *make mastery of correct spelling practically effortless.* Today you conquer once and for all time twenty-three new words that are frequently misspelled.

Another Confusing Ending

You think **-ance, -ence** is hard? There is an ending that is far worse, far more confusing, far more contradictory.

Which, for example, is correct: **depend*able*** or **depend*ible*, irrit*able*** or **irrit*ible*, indispens*able*** or **indispens*ible*, irresist*able*** or **irresist*ible*, inimit*able*** or **inimit*ible*?**

Here again, as in the previous section, we are fortunate: only five words with this confounding ending are generally misspelled. There is no reliable rule to keep you straight; there is no rhyme or reason that governs the correct choice. Each of the five demons has to be learned by itself but can be remembered quite easily by means of mnemonics.

1. **dependable:** An **able** man is depend**able**.
2. **indispensable:** An **able** man is indispens**able**.
3. **irresistible:** Women use lipstick to look irresistible. (The only vowel in **lipstick** is **i**.)
4. **irritable:** The verb is **irritate**.
5. **inimitable:** The verb is **imitate**.

Easy? Nothing to it. Study these mnemonics once again; then write the word that fits each definition:

unable to be imitated _____
able to be depended on _____
able to be irritated, grumpy _____
unable to be resisted _____
absolutely essential, cannot
  be dispensed with _____

And Still More Endings

The next problem is: when does a verb end in **-ify** and when does it end in **-efy**?

And the answer is: every common English verb which allows of such a choice ends in **-ify** except four archdemons that even the most educated writers are likely to come a cropper on: **liquefy, rarefy, stupefy, putrefy.**

Rarely, if ever, will you find a person who spells these words correctly, or even *doubts* that he is spelling them correctly when he misspells them. (Try your friends on the four words; stubborn souls will bet money that the incorrect form is correct!)

So practice on, and remember these four exceptions:

liquefy _____
rarefy _____
stupefy _____
putrefy _____

End every other word with **-ify**: **classify, testify, clarify, edify, mortify,** etc.

Of course, derived forms of the four verbs also use an **e** where you might expect an **i**: **liquefied, liquefaction; rarefied, rarefaction; stupefied, stupefaction; putrefied, putrefaction;** etc.

Special Memory-association Tricks

The ability to spell correctly is dependent on *memory, habit,* and *educated vision*. First, you must remember the precise combination of letters that make up a word. Then you must use that combination so often that it becomes an automatic process, requiring no thought, no figuring out. And finally, every other combination, no matter how close or similar, must *look* utterly wrong.

Apply these three cardinal principles in mastering the following twenty-nine frequently misspelled words. Examine each demon carefully, focusing your attention on the boldface letters that highlight the areas where most people fall into error. Study the mnemonic that will fix the correct pattern in your memory. Look at the complete word again. Then conceal the spelling and write the word on a sheet of paper, so that you begin to develop the habit of using only the correct pattern.

1. **all right.** Always two words, no matter what the meaning. Think of the opposite: **all wrong.**
2. **inoculate.** Think of its synonym **inject,** which also has only one **n,** one **c.**
3. **battalion.** Engages in **battle** — two **t**'s, one **l.**
4. **fricassee.** May be cooked in a **casserole** — one **c,** two **s**'s.
5. **anoint.** We anoint with **an oil** — one **n** only before the **o.**
6. **embarrassed.** Two robbers were embarrassed in Sing Sing — two **r**'s (two robbers), two **s**'s (Sing Sing).
7. **repetition.** Think of **repeat** — **e** (not **i**) follows the **p.**
8. **recommend.** This is the verb **commend** plus the prefix **re-;** hence one **c,** two **m**'s.
9. **drunkenness.** The adjective **drunken** (as in *a drunken bum*) plus the usual noun ending, **-ness** — hence two **n**'s where most people incorrectly use only one.
10. **tyranny.** Think of the phrase *Down with tyrants!* which has one **r,** two **n**'s.

11. **category.** The synonym **section** will remind you to use **e** where the untrained speller by error writes **a**.

12. **occasional.** One s, not two, by analogy with **treasure, measure, pleasure,** etc., all of which have the same sound for the single s.

13. **separate.** Look for a *rat*, thus avoiding the common incorrect form **seperate**.

14. **comparative.** Again look for a *rat*, to avoid the common misspelling **comparitive**.

Let us stop halfway for study and practice. Here are the first fourteen words correctly spelled, with the troublesome areas highlighted. Look at them once again, thus educating your vision; recall the mnemonic for each (**all right—all wrong, inoculate—inject,** etc.), thus educating your memory; and then write the word correctly in the blank to the right, thus educating your muscles.

all right	_____
inoculate	_____
battalion	_____
battalion	_____
fricassee	_____
anoint	_____
embarrassed	_____
repetition	_____
recommend	_____
drunkenness	_____
tyranny	_____
category	_____
occasional	_____
separate	_____
comparative	_____

EIGHTEENTH DAY

And Still More Tricks

Another fifteen words you can conquer through mnemonics.

More Mnemonics

And now we turn to the last fifteen demons that can be best and most quickly conquered by means of mnemonics.

15. **iridescent.** This word, meaning *displaying colors like a rainbow*, should remind you of the **iris**, the colored portion of the eye. Both **iris** and **rainbow** have only one **r**.
16. **vilify.** This verb means to call someone **vile** — hence one **l**.
17. **disappoint. Appoint** plus the prefix **dis-** — hence one **s**, two **p**'s.
18. **disappear.** As above, **appear** plus **dis-** — hence again one **s**, two **p**'s.
19. **dissipate.** This word is entirely different, and can be remembered by analogy with the previous two words precisely because it *is* different — two **s**'s one **p**, with an **i** in between.
20. **ecstasy: sy** (sigh) with **ecstasy** — an atrocious pun, but a wonderfully helpful mnemonic to remind you that the correct ending is **-sy**, not **-cy**.
21. **exhilarated.** If you feel **exhilarated**, you're often **hilarious**; both words come from the same root, and both have **la** after the **hi**.
22. **coolly.** Just add the adverbial ending **-ly** to **cool**, hence two **l**'s.
23. **vicious.** Think of the allied word **vice**, and you will be able to resist the temptation to misspell it **viscious**.
24. **balloon.** This is usually round, like a **ball** — hence two **l**'s.

25. **vacuum.** Means *emptiness,* or *vacant space;* like **vacant,** one c only.

26. **sacrilegious.** This word is opposite in a sense to **religious;** hence the **e** and **i** are in opposite order. Do not write sac-religious.

27. **grammar.** Don't let poor gram*mar mar* your speech.

28. **definitely.** Think of *definition* — hence **i,** not **a,** follows the **n.**

29. **descendant.** Every *descend*ant has an an*cestor* — hence -ant, not -ent.

Practice as before:

iridescent _____
vilify _____
disappoint _____
disappear _____
dissipate _____
ecstasy _____
exhilarated _____
coolly _____
vicious _____
balloon _____
vacuum _____
sacrilegious _____
grammar _____
definitely _____
descendant _____

By now you should have full control over these twenty-nine confusing words and should have no difficulty when you meet some of them in the test on page 90.

Let's Unconfuse These Confusing Pairs

Stationary and **stationery** are pronounced identically; so are **principal** and **principle.** How do you know which spelling to use when? Mnemonics will again come to your rescue.

Stationery consists of **paper** and other things for writing; the **-er** of **paper** tells you to spell it **station*er*y**. **Stationary,** on the other hand, means *standing in one place;* the **a** of **standing** and **place** tells you to spell it **station*ary***.

A **principle** is a *rule*; hence **-le** at the end. We try to live by ethical **principles,** we follow certain spelling **principles,** etc. **Principal,** on the other hand, is either an adjective meaning *main,* or a noun meaning *main person, thing, or amount*; and the **a** of *main* reminds you to use **-al.** For example, New York is the **principal** (main) seaport of the east coast; the **principal** of a school is the *main teacher*; the **principals** of a play are the *main actors*; and your **principal** in the bank is the *main amount* on which interest is paid.

Now do you have these four words properly unconfused? Then check the correct form in each sentence.

1. His (**principal, principle**) business is selling shoes.
2. The (**principal, principle**) of the school banks his money where 3¼ per cent is paid on the (**principal, principle**).
3. He is having new (**stationary, stationery**) printed.
4. A (**stationary, stationery**) object does not move.
5. He is a man of (**principal, principle**).

Check your results: 1-principal; 2-principal, principal; 3-stationery; 4-stationary; 5-principle.

Where to Dot Your i's

To learn, once and for all, when to write **ie** and when to write **ei** is relatively simple. It is based on the following rhymne, which you probably know:

> *I* before *e*
> Except after *c*
> Or when sounded like *a*
> As in *neighbor* or *weigh*.

Thus we use **-ei** in words like the following because the

immediately preceding letter is **c**: **receive, receipt, ceiling, conceive, conceit, deceive,** etc.

But we write **-ie** in words like the following, where the immediately preceding letter is *not* **c**: **believe, niece, siege, field, achieve, piece, brief,** etc.

What, no exceptions? But of course—and the exceptions cause the most grief. Study and practice the following:

seize _____
seizure _____
leisure _____
weird _____
sheik _____
financier _____

Keep these six words in mind, become accustomed to their appearance, and you'll have no trouble deciding where to put the **e**'s and **i**'s. (**Either** and **neither** also violate the rule, as do **ancient** and **conscience,** but few people misspell them.)

One Last Word

Let's wind up with a word that even the most sophisticated speller is likely to misspell. That word is the name for the small Hawaiian guitar—the one beginning with **uk-**. How would you spell it? Write it in the following blank before we go on: _____

Ten to one you wrote **ukelele.** Now ask some of your friends. You may get all sorts of weird combinations, but **ukelele** is the *incorrect* pattern most frequently found.

What is correct? Believe it or not, **ukulele!** Watch that second **u**—no other spelling is acceptable.

A Final Test of Your Learning

Now we are ready to make a new test of your ability as a speller. A random selection of thirty-four of the special demons we have discussed appears below—some correctly spelled, some as they are usually misspelled. Your job is to decide, without hesitation or confusion, which is which. If a word is correct, put a check (√) in the space provided; if it is incorrect, rewrite it correctly.

1. irridescent _____
2. inimitible _____
3. putrify _____
4. superintendant _____
5. tyranny _____
6. ecstacy _____
7. indispensable _____
8. dependant _____
9. descendant _____
10. vilify _____
11. proceed _____
12. sacreligious _____
13. inoculate _____
14. embarrassed _____
15. anoint _____
16. occassional _____
17. perseverance _____
18. achieve _____
19. drunkeness _____
20. dissapoint _____
21. supercede _____
22. ukelele _____
23. coolly _____
24. irresistable _____
25. disappate _____
26. occurence _____
27. seperate _____
28. seize _____
29. alright _____
30. definately _____
31. neice _____
32. wierd _____
33. liquefy _____
34. receive _____

Check your results: 1-iridescent; 2-inimitable; 3-putrefy; 4-superintendent; 5-√; 6-ecstasy; 7-√; 8-dependent; 9-√; 10-√; 11-√; 12-sacrilegious; 13-√; 14-√; 15-√; 16-occasional; 17-√; 18-√; 19-drunkenness; 20-disappoint; 21-supersede; 22-ukulele; 23-√; 24-irresistible; 25-dissipate; 26-occurrence; 27-separate; 28-√; 29-all right; 30-definitely; 31-niece; 32-weird; 33-√; 34-receive.

NINETEENTH DAY

Some More Spelling Tests to Keep You Alert

By now you should really feel your spelling ability improving—but don't relax. The next five tests will check on your learning and introduce some new demons for you to conquer.

Test 1

This is a most devilish and inconsiderate way to test your spelling powers. Probably if you were asked right out to spell any of the fifteen words below, you could do so without error. But in order really to test your ability, the words are distributed in groups of three, and in each group only *one* word is *misspelled*. If you can find that one in three groups and spell it correctly, your ability is average; if you can do it in all five you can be proud of yourself.

1. (a) disippate; (b) absence; (c) assassin _____
2. (a) assistant; (b) ukulele; (c) truely _____
3. (a) coolly; (b) newstand; (c) drunkenness _____
4. (a) suppress; (b) dumfound; (c) baloon _____
5. (a) benifit; (b) connoisseur; (c) ecstasy _____

Check your results: 1-a (dissipate); 2-c (truly); 3-b (newsstand); 4-c (balloon); 5-a (benefit).

Test 2

Of the following twenty words, exactly ten are misspelled. Identify the improper forms and spell them correctly.

1. unpredictible   _____
2. developement   _____
3. yield   _____
4. occassion   _____
5. privilege   _____
6. committee   _____
7. embarassed   _____
8. superintendant   _____
9. announce   _____
10. desparately   _____
11. attendance   _____
12. cargoes   _____
13. reccomend   _____
14. feminine   _____
15. dependible   _____
16. resistent   _____
17. hazzard   _____
18. raccoon   _____
19. professor   _____
20. gaiety   _____

Check your results. 1-unpredictable; 2-development; 4-occasion; 7-embarrassed; 8-superintendent; 10-desperately; 13-recommend; 15-dependable; 16-resistant; 17-hazard.

Test 3

Oddly enough, it's not the obscure word that causes the most trouble, but the common everyday word—the word that looks reasonable and correct no matter in which of two popular ways you write it.

Here is a test that will check your familiarity with the correct forms of commonly misspelled words. Two patterns are offered, and it is up to you to check the proper form. Fourteen to fifteen right is remarkable; eleven to thirteen, good; nine or ten, average.

1. (a) existence; (b) existance _____
2. (a) beginning; (b) begining _____
3. (a) foriegn; (b) foreign _____
4. (a) buisness; (b) business _____
5. (a) conceivable; (b) concievable _____
6. (a) dispatching; (b) despatching _____
7. (a) holliday; (b) holiday _____
8. (a) differant; (b) different _____
9. (a) phenomenal; (b) phenominal _____
10. (a) aggreed; (b) agreed _____
11. (a) liesurly; (b) leisurely _____
12. (a) disapear; (b) disappear _____
13. (a) labeled; (b) labled _____
14. (a) benificial; (b) beneficial _____
15. (a) femenine; (b) feminine _____

Check your results: 1-a, 2-a, 3-b, 4-b, 5-a, 6-a, 7-b, 8-b, 9-a, 10-b, 11-b, 12-b, 13-a, 14-b, 15-b.

Test 4

In each line, one word is purposely misspelled. It's up to you to find the error and correct it. Six right is average; seven to eight, good; nine to ten, superior.

1. (a) all right; (b) recommend; (c) innoculate _____
2. (a) holiday; (b) arguement; (c) absence _____
3. (a) drunkeness; (b) coolly; (c) grammar _____
4. (a) supercede; (b) definitely; (c) repetition _____
5. (a) dissipate; (b) pronounciation; (c) superintendent _____
6. (a) irresistable; (b) insistent; (c) category _____
7. (a) license; (b) exhilarate; (c) embarassing _____
8. (a) ecstacy; (b) benefited; (c) whiskey _____
9. (a) genealogy; (b) picnicer; (c) sergeant _____
10. (a) developement; (b) ukulele; (c) receive _____

Check your results: 1-c inoculate; 2-b argument; 3-a drunkenness; 4-a supersede; 5-b pronunciation; 6-a irresistible; 7-c embarrassing; 8-a ecstasy; 9-b picnicker; 10-a development.

Test 5

Here are twenty real demons—half spelled correctly and half spelled as many of us, alas, think they're spelled. Can you recognize the ten that are incorrect and spell them correctly?

1. peaceable
2. irritible
3. defense
4. surprise
5. sherrif
6. grammar
7. preceed
8. accoustics
9. kidnaped
10. concientious
11. insistant
12. developement
13. vicious
14. supersede
15. whiskey
16. repitition
17. suddeness
18. likable
19. trafficking
20. definately

Check your results: 2-irritable; 5-sheriff; 7-precede; 8-acoustics; 10-conscientious; 11-insistent; 12-development; 16-repetition; 17-suddenness; 20-definitely.

TWENTIETH DAY

A Final Acid Test of Your Newly Acquired Spelling Skill

When you've mastered all of the hundred words tested in this chapter, you'll be sure of one thing: it will be a cold day in August before anyone can stump you again!

Test 1: Elementary

Get all twenty-five right to prove your spelling contains no hint of illiteracy. Check the correct forms:

1. (a) too; (b) to (He is getting ____ fat.) ____
2. (a) it's; (b) its (It spent ____ power.) ____
3. (a) their; (b) there (They took off ____ coats.) ____
4. (a) grammer; (b) grammar ____
5. (a) amoung; (b) among ____
6. (a) receive; (b) recieve ____
7. (a) therefore; (b) therefor (consequently) ____
8. (a) immediately; (b) imediatly ____
9. (a) buisness; (b) business ____
10. (a) seperate; (b) separate ____
11. (a) benefit; (b) benifit ____
12. (a) lose; (b) loose (We will ____ money.) ____
13. (a) untill; (b) until ____
14. (a) doesn't; (b) dosen't ____
15. (a) coming; (b) comming ____
16. (a) ocurred; (b) occurred ____
17. (a) neccessary; (b) necessary ____
18. (a) existence; (b) existance ____
19. (a) appeerence; (b) appearance ____

20. (a) accross; (b) across ____
21. (a) discription; (b) description ____
22. (a) your; (b) you're (Is that what ____ doing?) ____
23. (a) supprise; (b) surprise ____
24. (a) weird; (b) wierd ____
25. (a) friend; (b) frend ____

Check your results: 1-a, 2-b, 3-a, 4-b, 5-b, 6-a, 7-a, 8-a, 9-b, 10-b, 11-a, 12-a, 13-b, 14-a, 15-a, 16-b, 17-b, 18-a, 19-b, 20-b, 21-b, 22-b, 23-b, 24-a, 25-a.

Test 2: Intermediate

Get at least twenty-one right to feel that your spelling is better than average; seventeen right to grade it average.

1. (a) occassion; (b) occasion ____
2. (a) villain; (b) villian ____
3. (a) acommodate; (b) accommodate ____
4. (a) occurrence; (b) occurrance ____
5. (a) truely; (b) truly ____
6. (a) fourty; (b) forty ____
7. (a) pursue; (b) persue ____
8. (a) arguement; (b) argument ____
9. (a) dissappear; (b) disappear ____
10. (a) dissappoint; (b) disappoint ____
11. (a) neice; (b) niece ____
12. (a) privilege; (b) priviledge ____
13. (a) alright; (b) all right ____
14. (a) desireable; (b) desirable ____
15. (a) addresses; (b) addreses ____
16. (a) dispair; (b) despair ____
17. (a) definitely; (b) definately ____
18. (a) developement; (b) development ____
19. (a) irresistible; (b) irresistable ____
20. (a) sargeant; (b) sergeant ____
21. (a) noticable; (b) noticeable ____
22. (a) lonelyness; (b) loneliness ____

23. (a) vengance; (b) vengeance _____
24. (a) procede; proceed _____
25. (a) conscientious; (b) concientious _____

Check your results: 1-b, 2-a, 3-b, 4-a, 5-b, 6-b, 7-a, 8-b, 9-b, 10-b, 11-b, 12-a, 13-b, 14-b, 15-a, 16-b, 17-a, 18-b, 19-a, 20-b, 21-b, 22-b, 23-b, 24-b, 25-a.

Test 3: Advanced

Get twenty or more right and you may confidently boast that your spelling is downright good; get all twenty-five right to label your ability excellent. Check the correct forms:

1. (a) batallion; (b) battalion _____
2. (a) disasterous; (b) disastrous _____
3. (a) embarassing; (b) embarrassing _____
4. (a) benefited; (b) benefitted _____
5. (a) balloon; (b) baloon _____
6. (a) rythmical; rhythmical _____
7. (a) indispensible; (b) indispensable _____
8. (a) sacrilegious; (b) sacreligious _____
9. (a) superintendant; (b) superintendent _____
10. (a) passtime; (b) pastime _____
11. (a) parallel; (b) paralell _____
12. (a) exhilaration; (b) exhillaration _____
13. (a) irrelevant; (b) irrelevent _____
14. (a) tyrranize; (b) tyrannize _____
15. (a) repetition, (b) repitition _____
16. (a) perseverance; (b) perseverence _____
17. (a) grievious; (b) grievous _____
18. (a) irritible; (b) irritable _____
19. (a) reccomend; (b) recommend _____
20. (a) rediculous; (b) ridiculous _____
21. (a) acceed; (b) accede _____
22. (a) cooly; (b) coolly _____
23. (a) supercede; (b) supersede _____
24. (a) absence; (b) abscence _____
25. (a) anoint; (b) annoint _____

Check your results: 1-b, 2-b, 3-b, 4-a, 5-a, 6-b, 7-b, 8-a, 9-b, 10-b, 11-a, 12-a, 13-a, 14-b, 15-a, 16-a, 17-b, 18-b, 19-b, 20-b, 21-b, 22-b, 23-b, 24-a, 25-a.

Test 4: Postgraduate

Get all twenty-five right, and you are undoubtedly a perfect speller, or get at least twenty right to claim that you are practically perfect. Check the correct forms:

1. (a) eliptical; (b) elliptical _____
2. (a) dissipation; (b) disippation _____
3. (a) ecstasy; (b) ecstacy _____
4. (a) ukulele; (b) ukelele _____
5. (a) khaki; (b) kahki _____
6. (a) innoculate; (b) inoculate _____
7. (a) drunkeness; (b) drunkenness _____
8. (a) insistant; (b) insistent _____
9. (a) persistant; (b) persistent _____
10. (a) corroborate; (b) corobborate _____
11. (a) vaccilate; (b) vacillate _____
12. (a) dilletante; (b) dilettante _____
13. (a) panicy; (b) panicky _____
14. (a) vaccuum; (b) vacuum _____
15. (a) plebian; (b) plebeian _____
16. (a) tariff; (b) tarrif _____
17. (a) sheriff; (b) sherrif _____
18. (a) connoisseur; (b) conoisseur _____
19. (a) naïveté; (b) naivety _____
20. (a) accelerator; (b) accelerater _____
21. (a) broccoli; (b) brocolli _____
22. (a) racoon; (b) raccoon _____
23. (a) catarrh; (b) cattarrh _____
24. (a) pleurisy; (b) pleurasy _____
25. (a) irridescent; (b) iridescent _____

Check your results: 1-b, 2-a, 3-a, 4-a, 5-a, 6-b, 7-b, 8-b, 9-b, 10-a, 11-a, 12-b, 13-b, 14-b, 15-b, 16-a, 17-a, 18-a, 19-a, 20-a, 21-a, 22-b, 23-a, 24-a, 25-b.

TWENTY-FIRST DAY

Just for Fun

Do Words Confuse You?

One of the basic steps that a person often takes in learning a new word involves a normal sense of confusion between its actual meaning and its opposite meaning. Below you will find fifteen important and valuable words, each followed by a phrase which is either essentially the *same* (S) or more nearly *opposite* (O) in meaning to the key word. It's up to you to decide which is which. Par on this test is nine correct decisions. How well can *you* do?

1. **enervated:** exhausted, worn out ____
2. **sacrilegious:** excessively pious or God-fearing ____
3. **abject:** full of haughtiness ____
4. **adulation:** overabundant flattery ____
5. **dearth:** great deficiency ____
6. **carnivorous:** avoiding meat ____
7. **convivial:** grumpy and unsociable ____
8. **insidious:** working secretly or subtly ____
9. **expiate:** atone for ____
10. **frugality:** unnecessary extravagance ____
11. **indolent:** full of ambition and energy ____
12. **senile:** mentally and physically weak from old age ____
13. **verbose:** unusually quiet, using few words ____
14. **parsimonious:** miserly, overly economical ____
15. **suave:** smoothly agreeable or polite ____

Check your results: 1-S, 2-O, 3-O, 4-S, 5-S, 6-O, 7-O, 8-S, 9-S, 10-O, 11-O, 12-S, 13-O, 14-S, 15-S.

How Is Your Pronunciation?

When you use a word, do you generally pronounce it according to "educated standards?" Test yourself by checking what you consider the correct pronunciation of each of eighteen words below. A phenomenal score is seventeen to eighteen right; excellent, thirty to sixteen; good, nine to twelve; average, six to eight. How high can *you* score?

1. **canapé** (an appetizer): (a) kə-NAYP'; (b) ka-na-PAY' ____
2. **asphalt** (a kind of paving): (a) ASS'-fawlt; (b) ASH'-fawlt ____
3. **zoology** (the science of animals): (a) zoe-OL'-ə-jee; (b) zoo-OL'-ə-jee ____
4. **dour** (*stern, severe*): (a) to rhyme with *poor;* (b) to rhyme with *hour* ____
5. **obesity** (*excessive weight*): (a) o-BEE'-sə-tee; (b) o-BESS'-ə-tee ____
6. **respite** (*a pause*): (a) RES'-pit; (b) rə-SPITE' ____
7. **thyme** (*a flavoring*): (a) TIME; (b) THIME ____
8. **efficacy** (*effectiveness*): (a) ə-FICK'-ə-see; (b) EFF'-ə-kə-see ____
9. **regime** (*a system*): (a) rə-ZHEEM' (zh is the sound of s in **pleasure**); (b) rə-JEEM' ____
10. **scourge** (*an affliction*): (a) SKURJ; (b) SKORJ ____
11. **sachet** (*a scent bag*): (a) SASH'-et; (b) sa-SHAY' ____
12. **indefatigable** (*tireless*): (a) in-də-FAT'-ə-gə-bəl; (b) in-də-fə-TEEG'-ə-bəl ____
13. **antarctic** (*a region*): (a) ant-AR'-tic; (b) ant-ARK'-tic ____
14. **trespasser** (*encroacher*): (a) tress-PASS'-ər; (b) TRESS'-pə-sər ____
15. **viscount** (*a nobleman*): (a) VYE'-kount; (b) VIS'-kount ____
16. **alias** (*an assumed name*): (a) ə-LYE'-əs; (b) AY'-lee-əs ____

17. **chameleon** (*an animal*): (a) CHAM′-ə-lon; (b) kə-MEE′-lee-ən ____

18. **clandestine** (*secret*): (a) klan-DES′-tin; (b) KLAN′-də-styne ____

Check your results: 1-b, 2-a, 3-a, 4-a, 5-a, 6-a, 7-a, 8-b, 9-a, 10-a, 11-b, 12-a, 13-b, 14-b, 15-a, 16-b, 17-b, 18-a.

Around the Alphabet — and Back Again

Do words come to you quickly? If a word is offered to you, can you immediately respond with another of essentially opposite meaning?

This is an acid test of the speed and accuracy of your verbal reactions. For each key word below, write another of essentially opposite meaning, beginning with the indicated letter. Allow yourself ten minutes—not a second more. Par for this course is thirty right; expert rating, forty. How well can *you* do?

1. purposely — a_____
2. harmful — b_____
3. expensive — c_____
4. wet — d_____
5. calm — e_____
6. to sink — f_____
7. harsh — g_____
8. low — h_____
9. genius — i_____
10. solemn — j_____
11. to relinquish — k_____
12. careful — l_____
13. phobia — m_____
14. synthetic — n_____
15. transparent — o_____
16. to reward — p_____
17. agreement — q_____

18. slow   r_____
19. land   s_____
20. permanent   t_____
21. above   u_____
22. occupied   v_____
23. ruddy   w_____
24. today   y_____
25. straight   z_____
26. indifferent   z_____
27. white of egg y_____
28. strong   w_____
29. silent   v_____
30. commonplace   u_____
31. practice   t_____
32. frivolous   s_____
33. conformist   r_____
34. answer   q_____
35. intersecting p_____
36. young   o_____
37. both   n_____
38. to magnify   m_____
39. infinite   l_____
40. dull   k_____
41. safety   j_____
42. soiled   i_____
43. sickness   h_____
44. to disperse   g_____
45. mute   f_____
46. altruist   e_____
47. sure   d_____
48. unusual   c_____
49. long   b_____
50. enemy   a_____

Check your results: 1-accidentally; 2-beneficial; 3-cheap, complimentary; 4-dry, desiccated; 5-excited, excitable, emotional, effervescent, ebullient; 6-float; 7-gentle, genial, gracious; 8-high, hilly; 9-idiot, imbecile; 10-jolly, jesting, jocose, jocund, joking, joyful, joyous, jovial; 11-keep; 12-lax, loose; 13-mania; 14-natural; 15-opaque, obscure; 16-punish, punishment, penalty, penalize, penance; 17-quarrel; 18-rapid; 19-sea; 20-temporary; 21-under, underneath; 22-vacant; 23-wan, waxy; 24-yesterday, yore; 25-zigzag; 26-zealous; 27-yolk; 28-weak, wasted, withered, worn; 29-verbose, voluble, vociferous; 30-unusual, uncommon, unique, unprecedented; 31-theory; 32-serious, sincere, sedate, solemn, staid; 33-rebel, revolutionary, resister; 34-question, query, quiz; 35-parallel; 36-old, obsolete; 37-neither, none; 38-minimize; 39-limited; 40-keen, knifelike; 41-jeopardy; 42-immaculate; 43-health, haleness, hardiness; 44-gather; 45-fluent, forensic; 46-egoist, egotist, egocentric, egomaniac; 47-doubtful, dubious, debatable, disbelieving, distrustful; 48-common, commonplace, conventional, customary, current; 49-brief; 50-ally.

PART V

Speak Correctly

Correct usage, no matter how you slice it, is what most educated people say and write. The rules of English grammar that are unselfconsciously observed by effective speakers, by those who have the public ear, and by professional and established authors, are the ones that are important.

In Part V you will consider and thoroughly drill on three categories of these important rules—categories that account for 75 per cent of the errors made by unsophisticated speakers.

TWENTY-SECOND DAY

An English Test for You

Let's find out if your everyday English is as good as you are.

Are You Better Than Your English Says You Are?

When you speak to schoolmates or to teachers and other adults, when you get up to address the class, when you go out to look for a job, when you meet someone for the first time, or when you write a letter or report that will be read by people whose judgment of your knowledge and intelligence is important to you—at such times does your command of language do you full justice, or does it sometimes fail to help you make the kind of impression you are potentially capable of making?

Test Yourself

When it comes to first impressions, it seems that the old saying is frequently reversed: at the beginning, at least, words speak louder than actions. That's when the English you use can be an asset—or a stumbling block in the way of acceptance. Which is it in your case?

To find out whether your English works for or against you, take this revealing test. In each sentence, check off the word you would be most likely to use in your own speech or writing.

1. Let's just keep this a secret between you and (I, me).
2. The position will be offered to either you or (me, I).
3. We found everyone home except (he, him) and his father.
4. If I were (she, her), I wouldn't act that way.
5. I know you're taller than (I, me).
6. They can work a lot faster than (we, us).
7. Call Mrs. Brown or (I, me) whenever you need help.
8. (Who, Whom) do you expect will be appointed chairman of the dance committee next year?
9. (Who, Whom) are you waiting for?
10. The prisoner was (hanged, hung) at dawn.
11. How did his speech (affect, effect) you?
12. It was the most beautiful (affect, effect) we had ever seen.
13. Don't sound so (**incredulous, incredible**); what I'm saying is absolutely true.
14. That job is very difficult; (beside, besides), I'm not really trained for it.
15. Why don't you (lay, lie) down for a nap before dinner?
16. (Lie, Lay) your hand on the radiator and see how hot it is.
17. The book reports (lay, laid) on the teacher's desk all morning.
18. Has the cat (laid, lain) here all morning?
19. (Has, Have) either of your parents come in yet?
20. Neither of your suggestions (is, are) really practical.
21. Every one of his answers (is, are) correct.
22. Either the principal or his secretary (are, is) in the office at all times.
23. The cost of loose-leaf sheets (are, is) rising again.
24. How (is, are) your mother and father feeling?
25. (These, This) phenomena (are, is) worth seeing.

Check your results: 1-me; 2-me; 3-him; 4-she; 5-I; 6-we; 7-me; 8-Who; 9-Whom; 10-hanged; 11-affect; 12-effect; 13-incredulous; 14-besides; 15-lie; 16-lay; 17-lay; 18-lain; 19-Has; 20-is; 21-is; 22-is; 23-is; 24-are; 25-These, are.

A score of twenty-three to twenty-five correct is excellent; nineteen to twenty-two, good; thirteen to eighteen, fair; twelve or less, poor.

Let's Get Down to Work

How did you do? Don't feel dismayed if you made an incorrect choice in a great many of the sentences. For although the English language is full of traps for the unwary, you will be amazed at how quickly and successfully you can learn to avoid the main pitfalls and booby traps of correct usage. You can master the material in this part of the book in just a few days. But within those few days you can take giant strides forward in improving your English, discover and permanently root out most of the errors you now make, and gain self-assurance whenever you speak or write.

How can we expect our work to be so easy and so immediately rewarding? Because 75 per cent or more of the common errors made in grammar occur in just three broad areas of usage: (1) pronouns (**I, you, me, him,** etc.); (2) the words **lay** and **lie**; (3) singular and plural words. In Part V, most of our attention will be devoted to these areas. Let us start with the pronouns.

All About Pronouns

PROBLEM 1: Shall we keep this strictly between **you and I** —or between **you and me?**

SOLUTION: Probably the most common error made by people who are not quite sure of their grammar occurs in the use of the pronoun following **between**. After this word, and also after **except** and **but** (all of which are prepositions), only the pronouns below are grammatically acceptable.

RULE 1. Use these object pronouns after the prepositions **between, except,** and **but: me, him, her, us, them.**

Read the following phrases aloud, getting used to their sound in your ears and their feel on your tongue:

between you and me
between him and her
between them and us

no one except him
all but me
everyone but her

PROBLEM 2: Do you want both Paul and I—or Paul and **me** —to come in early tomorrow?

SOLUTION: The choice of the correct word becomes particularly confusing when we have a combination of two pronouns or of a noun and a pronoun. Consider these sentences:

1. This is for you and (**I, me**).
2. Are you inviting Mary and (**we, us**) to your party?
3. That's no way to treat (**we, us**) boys.
4. George and (**he, him**) will come in late tomorrow.
5. Do you want (**he and I, him and me**) to help you?

Whenever you find yourself in this kind of trouble, you can apply an easy, and foolproof, rule: Omit, for a moment, the additional word with which the pronoun is combined, and you will unerringly make the proper choice.

In sentence 1, omit **you**. We would naturally say "This is for **me**"—hence "This is for you and **me**."

In sentence 2, omit **Mary**. We have to say "Are you inviting **us** to your party?"—hence "Are you inviting Mary and **us**?"

In sentence 3, omit **boys**. "That's no way to treat **us**"—hence "**us** boys."

In sentence 4, omit **George**. "**He** will come in late tomorrow"—hence "George and **he** will come in late tomorrow."

In sentence 5, take **one** of the pronouns at a time. "Do you want **him** to help you?" "Do you want **me** to help you?" —hence "Do you want **him** and me to help you?"

RULE 2: To figure out the correct pronoun to use in a combination, temporarily omit one part of the combination.

PROBLEM 3. Are you taller than **me**—or taller than **I**? And do you eat as much as **me**—or as much as **I**?

SOLUTION: Tuck the words **than** and **as** away in a corner of your mind. To figure out the correct pronoun to use after either of these two connecting words (called conjunctions), just finish your sentence by adding the understood verb:

1. Are you taller than (**me, I**) am?
2. Do you eat as much as (**me, I**) do?
3. You can't type as fast as (**she, her**) does.
4. We're not as rich as (**them, they**) are.

In sentence 1 and sentence 2, the correct form is **I**. In sentence 3 it is **she**, and in sentence 4 **they**.

RULE 3: To figure out the correct pronoun to use after **than** and **as**, fill in the missing verb.

PROBLEM 4: When someone on the phone asks for Miss Brown, and *you* are Miss Brown, what should you say: "This is **she**" or "This is **her**"?

SOLUTION: We have an example, here, of one of the most recurrent—and most annoying—of pronoun problems. It was **he**—or **him**? It could have been **she**—or **her**? If you were **I**—or **me**?

To solve your dilemma in these instances, you must become familiar with the important forms of the verb **to be**: **is, are, am; was, were; have, has, had been.**

And then, in addition, you need only bear in mind that the following subject pronouns are correctly used after any of these forms of the verb **to be**: **I, he, she, we, they.**

Get used to the sound of these sentences:

1. This is **she**.
2. It was **he** who did it.
3. If you were **I**, wouldn't you act the same way?
4. It is **they** I'm referring to — not you.

RULE 4: After any form of the verb **to be**, use the subject pronouns **I, he, she, we, they**. However, "It's **me**," though not technically correct, is usually acceptable in informal conversation.

PROBLEM 5: **Who** are you talking to, or **whom** are you talking to? **Who** do you see, or **whom** do you see? Is this the only person **who**—or **whom**—you feel you can trust?

SOLUTION: **Who** and **whom** are treacherous and bothersome pronouns, and there's no point in pretending otherwise. But you can avoid all the confusion that these demons usually cause by applying one simple principle.

RULE 5: Whenever you feel any doubt about whether to use **who** or **whom**, turn the sentence around so that you can substitute **he** or **him**. If **he** fits, the correct word is **who**; if, **him** fits, the correct word is **whom**.

For example, in the sentences of our problem, the only sensible English, when we rearrange the word order, is as follows: You are talking to **him**, you see **him**, you feel you can trust **him**. In all three sentences then, only **whom** is the strictly correct form.

Study these:

1. (Who, Whom) is here? **He** is here — hence **who**.
2. (Who, Whom) do you know? You know him — hence **whom**.
3. (Who, Whom) are you calling? You're calling **him** — hence **whom**.
4. (Who, Whom) are you referring to? You are referring to **him** — hence **whom**.
5. (Who, Whom) do you think you are? You think you are **he** (you will recall that any form of the verb **to be** takes a subject pronoun)—hence **who**.

What do you have to know in order to be able to handle pronouns with correctness and assurance? Let us take a moment to summarize.

1. After any preposition, notably **between, except,** and but, use object pronouns (**me, him, her, us, them**).

2. After any form of the verb **to be,** use subject pronouns (**I, he, she, we, they**).

3. In combined forms (**he and I, Jane and us,** etc.), omit one element of the combination to determine whether to use a subject or object pronoun.

4. After the conjunctions **than** and **as,** fill in the understood verb.

5. To straighten yourself out on **who** and **whom,** substitute **he** or **him: who** stands for **he, whom** for **him.**

Ready for a test of your skill?

Check Your Learning

1. Let's just keep this betwen you and (**me, I**).
2. Was it (**he, him**) you were worried about?
3. If you were (**me, I**), what would you do?
4. I'm not as fast as (**him, he**).
5. They work a lot harder than (**us, we**).
6. I will call (**he, him**) and his wife tomorrow.
7. Was the letter addressed to you and (**me, I**)?
8. She is one woman (**who, whom**) I really admire.
9. (**Who, Whom**) did you come to see?
10. (**Who, Whom**) are you waiting for?
11. (**Who, Whom**) are you talking about?
12. (**Who, Whom**) would you like to be?

Check your results: 1-me; 2-he; 3-I; 4-he; 5-we; 6-him; 7-me; 8-whom; 9-Whom; 10-Whom; 11-Whom; 12-Who.

TWENTY-THIRD DAY

The Most Confusing Verbs in the English Language and How to Get Them Straight

> *No other verbs cause as much trouble as* **lay** *and* **lie**. *Now you can begin mastering them by learning a few simple and easy-to-apply principles.*

All About **lay** *and* **lie**

PROBLEM 6. Do you **lay** down—or **lie** down—for a nap before dinner?

SOLUTION: Although **lay** and **lie** are without doubt the most confusing—and confused—pair of verbs in the English language, and although they are a source of never-ending contradiction and bewilderment to many people, you can learn how to untangle them before you come to the end of the next page.

Understanding the distinction between **lay** and **lie** is child's play. Training yourself to observe this distinction whenever you speak will require a little more effort.

This is all you have to know: **lay** means *to place* or *put* something somewhere. **Lie** means *to recline, rest,* or *remain.*

Now you must admit that nothing could be simpler or more clear-cut than that.

You **lay** (*place*) a book on the table; you **lay** (*place*) a child in its crib; you **lay** (*put*) in a supply of coal.

You **lie** (*remain*) asleep; the penny was **lying** (*resting*) in the mud; you **lie** down (*recline*) for a nap.

Clear so far? But wait, it gets just a bit more complicated in the past and perfect tenses.

Today you **lie** down for a nap; yesterday you **lay** down for a nap (past tense); you **have lain** asleep all morning (perfect tense—the form used after **has, have,** or **had**).

It is in the past and perfect tenses that most of the errors are made, so study the previous paragraph until you understand it thoroughly. And memorize this simple line:

to recline, etc.: **lie, lay, have lain.**

The past and perfect tenses of **lay,** *to place,* offer no difficulty. Today you **lay** the book on the table; yesterday you **laid** it on the table (past tense); you **have laid** the book on the table (perfect tense).

Here is a final line to memorize, and then you will know everything there is to know about the verbs **lay** and **lie:**

to place, etc.: **lay, laid, have laid.**

Now read the following sentences aloud, get used to their sound, and understand precisely why each form is used:

lie:

Lie down, please. (*recline*)

The dog was **lying** on the sofa. (*reclining*)

Did you **lie** down for a nap after dinner? (*recline*)

He **lay** quietly while the doctor examined him. (*reclined,* past tense)

The report **has lain** on the president's desk all week. (*remained,* perfect tense)

lay:

Lay your hands on mine. (*place*)

Lay the child on its back. (*place*)

He **laid** his hand on mine. (*placed,* past tense)

He **has laid** my fears to rest. (*placed,* perfect tense)

Let us see how skillfully you can avoid **lay-lie** traps.

Check Your Learning
1. The dog is (**laying, lying**) on the sofa.
2. Why don't you (**lie, lay**) down for a short nap?
3. The wounded man (**laid, lay**) in the gutter.
4. She has (**lain, laid**) asleep all morning.
5. These items have (**lain, laid**) on the shelf all month.
6. Did you (**lie, lay**) on the beach last Sunday?

Check your results: 1-lying; 2-lie; 3-lay; 4-lain; 5-lain; 6-lie.

TWENTY-FOURTH DAY

Final Steps for Mastering *lay* and *lie*

Today you nail down your understanding of these troublesome verbs and prove to yourself that you can now avoid all confusion.

Mop-up on lay *and* lie

Easy so far? Then let's really nail the correct forms home so you'll never again be confused. **Lay**, I have said, means *put*; **lie** means *recline, rest,* or *remain*. The present participle of **lie** is, of course, **lying**; of **lay**, **laying**. Can you, then, zip through these ten sentences checking the correct word in each one?

1. When we (**lie, lay**) on the bed, we can feel the springs.
2. If you (**lie, lay**) away a few dollars every week, you will soon be able to buy that bicycle.
3. (**Lay, Lie**) still for a few minutes.
4. Don't (**lay, lie**) the books on that high shelf.
5. (**Lay, Lie**) your composition on my desk.
6. We found the wounded man (**laying, lying**) on the floor.
7. He is accustomed to (**laying, lying**) down for a short nap after dinner.
8. (**Lie, Lay**) the baby in its crib.
9. We saw a penny (**laying, lying**) in the mud.
10. He was (**laying, lying**) in bed watching television.

Check your results: 1-lie; 2-lay; 3-Lie; 4-lay; 5-lay; 6-lying; 7-lying; 8-Lay; 9-lying; 10-lying.

How About Past Tenses?

So now you may consider yourself an expert on the simple part of **lay** and **lie**. But how good are you in the past and perfect tenses, which are much harder? Before you do the next test, keep three points in mind:

1. The past of **lie** (*recline*, etc.) is **lay**. The past of **lay** (*put, place*) is **laid**. For example:

I **lay** in bed so long this morning, I was late for school.
I **laid** my clothes out the night before, so I was able to sleep ten minutes longer.

2. After the auxiliary verb **did**, use the present tense of **lie** (*recline*, etc.), and of **lay** (*put, place*). **Did** is a past-tense marker, and so the main verb should not be put in the past. For example:

Did you **lie** down? — No, I **did** not **lie** down.
Did you **lay** your clothes away? — No, I **did** not **lay** my clothes away.

3. The perfect tense of **lie** (*recline*) is **has, have,** or **had lain**. The perfect tense of **lay** (*put, place*) is **has, have,** or **had laid**. For example:

Has your mother **lain** down for a nap?
The baby **has lain** asleep for over three hours.
Have you **laid** your homework on Miss Brown's desk?

Test Yourself

I. Check the correct form:
1. She (**lay, laid**) down for a nap.
2. When she (**lay, laid**) down for a nap, her dinner burned.
3. She (**lay, laid**) the work aside for a few minutes.
4. The nurse (**lay, laid**) the patient on his back.
5. They (**lay, laid**) the foundation of the building.
6. He (**lay, laid**) quietly for a few minutes.

7. Did you (lay, lie) down for a nap?
8. Did you (lay, lie) the baby down?

II. Check the correct past participle:
1. Has he (laid, lain) here long?
2. Have you (laid, lain) away your woolens?
3. Had he (laid, lain) quietly, this would not have happened.
4. After he had (laid, lain) his books down, he sat down to dinner.
5. Has she (laid, lain) asleep all day?
6. Where have you (laid, lain) my things?
7. His crime has (laid, lain) on his conscience all year.
8. The diamond has (laid, lain) on his desk for months, and no one ever noticed it.

III. Now, as a general review, check the correct verb:
1. The patient is (lying, laying) down.
2. (Lie, Lay) the baby down.
3. Estelle has (laid, lain) down for a nap.
4. He picked up the sticks and (laid, lay) them straight.
5. We (laid, lay) in the sun all morning.
6. He (laid, lay) his hands on the controls, and waited for the signal to start.
7. Have you (laid, lain) away your summer clothing?
8. The bill has (laid, lain) on the president's desk all week.
9. Which shelf did you (lie, lay) the curtains on?
10. The diamond (laid, lay) in the gutter all day, and no one saw it.
11. Did you (lay, lie) on your back all night?
12. Let sleeping dogs (lay, lie).
13. He was (lying, laying) on the floor.
14. Let us (lay, lie) our plans carefully.
15. All morning, he (laid, lay) in wait.
16. (Lay, Lie) down, please.
17. (Lay, Lie) your hand on mine.
18. I won't (lay, lie) down.

19. I can't stand all this junk (**laying, lying**) around.

20. He loves to (**lay, lie**) in the sun and watch the ships pass by.

Check your results:

I. 1-lay; 2-lay; 3-laid; 4-laid; 5-laid; 6-lay; 7-lie; 8-lay.

II. 1-lain; 2-laid; 3-lain; 4-laid; 5-lain; 6-laid; 7-lain; 8-lain.

III. 1-lying; 2-lay; 3-lain; 4-laid; 5-lay; 6-laid; 7-laid; 8-lain; 9-lay; 10-lay; 11-lie; 12-lie; 13-lying; 14-lay; 15-lay; 16-lie; 17-lay; 18-lie; 19-lying; 20-lie.

TWENTY-FIFTH DAY

How to Find Your Way Through Singulars and Plurals

Do you have to stop sometimes and wonder whether to use **is** *or* **are,** **has** *or* **have,** **was** *or* **were**? *Let's discover how easy it is to decide, once you're sure of the rules.*

All About Singulars and Plurals

PROBLEM 7: Neither of his parents **is**—or **are**—alive?

SOLUTION: Ask yourself, what word is understood between **neither** and **of** in this problem sentence? Obviously the word **one**. And do we say, "Neither one **is**" or "Neither one **are**"? Equally obviously, **is**—hence "Neither of his parents is alive."

And here we have the important key we need to choose the verb that follows **neither of, either of,** and **one of.**

Can You Figure These Out?

1. Neither (**one**) of his parents (**has, have**) arrived.
2. Either (**one**) of the girls (**is, are**) capable of running the switchboard.
3. Each (**one**) of these reports (**was, were**) checked.
4. **One** of my best friends (**works, work**) in your department.

If you noted that we were talking about **one** in these problems, you select the *first* verb in each case: one **has,** one **is,** etc.

PROBLEM 8: **Has**—or **have**—the manager or his assistant come in yet? **Has**—or **have**—your mother and father arrived?

SOLUTION: In the first problem sentence, the correct verb is **has**; but in the second sentence, the correct verb is **have**. Why the difference? Note the rule that applies.

RULE 6: When two singular subjects are connected by **or** or **nor**, use a singular verb; when they are connected by **and**, use a plural verb.

Puzzle these out:

1. (**Has, Have**) either your son or daughter ever worked here?
2. (**Is, Are**) there a pen or pencil in the drawer?
3. Neither the mechanic nor his helper (**has, have**) come in yet.
4. (**Is, Are**) your son and daughter home today?
5. (**Was, Were**) the pen and pencil in the drawer?

Sentences 1 through 3 have singular subjects connected by **or** or **nor**, so the correct verbs are singular: **has, is, has**. In sentences 4 and 5, the connective is **and**, the verb is plural: **are, were**.

PROBLEM 9: **Is**—or **Are**—the cost of these items dropping?

SOLUTION: What is dropping, the **cost** or the **items**? It's the **cost** (singular), not the **items** (plural). Hence a *singular* verb is required. The correct answer: **is**.

RULE 7: When a singular subject is followed by **of** and a plural noun, ignore the word after **of**, and make your verb agree with the singular subject.

Puzzle these out:

1. A vase of flowers (**is, are**) standing on her desk.
2. The first batch of items (**was, were**) defective.
3. Another collection of orders (**has, have**) just come in.
4. The aim of our employees (**is, are**) to turn out more work.

121

In each instance, the subject (the word before **of**) is singular: **vase, batch, collection, aim.** Therefore the correct verb is also singular: **is, was, has, is.**

Troublesome Plurals

The following words do not end in **s**; nevertheless they are plurals and should be treated as such:

> **criteria** (singular **criterion**)
> **memoranda** (singular **memorandum**)
> **phenomena** (singular **phenomenon**)
> **data** (singular **datum**, rarely used)

Hence we correctly say **these criteria, those phenomena,** etc.

In the following words (double or hyphenated), we add the **s** to the main elements in order to pluralize them:

> mother-in-law, mothers-in-law
> passer-by, passers-by
> looker-on, lookers-on
> attorney general, attorneys general

But the plurals of solid words such as **spoonful, cupful, handful,** etc. are **spoonfuls, cupfuls, handfuls,** etc.

Are you ready, now, for a complete test of your understanding of singulars and plurals?

Check Your Learning

1. Neither of these reports (**are, is**) satisfactory.
2. If every one of the employees (**puts, put**) in some overtime, we can get the job done in a week.
3. Each of his children (**have, has**) managed to go to college.
4. Either the president or the vice-president (**has, have**) attended every meeting.
5. The greater size of these machines (**accounts, account**) for their staggering cost.

6. He and his sister (is, are) waiting to see you.
7. (Mother-in-laws, Mothers-in-law) are rarely as bad as they are painted.
8. (That, Those) criteria (is, are) no longer valid.

Check your results: 1-is; 2-puts; 3-has; 4-has; 5-accounts; 6-are; 7-Mothers-in-law; 8-Those, are.

Other Words Often Confused

let — leave. Let means *to permit*: **let** me go, **let's** not talk about it. **Leave** means *to go away*: **leave** the room, **leave** me alone.

hanged — hung. A person is **hanged** when he is put to death by hanging; a picture or other object (occasionally, a person) is **hung** when held suspended: The horse thief was **hanged**; they **hanged** the murderer at dawn; we **hung** the picture on the wall.

alumnus — alumna. A male graduate of a school is an **alumnus**, a female graduate an **alumna**. The plural of **alumnus** is **alumni** (a-LUM-nye); the plural of **alumna** is **alumnae** (a-LUM-nee).

incredible — incredulous. A story, thing, or person that *cannot be believed*—i.e., that is *unbelievable*—is **incredible**: an **incredible** account of the night's adventures, an **incredible** witness, etc. A person (and *only* a person) who is *skeptical, unwilling to believe,* is **incredulous**: He looked utterly **incredulous** when he heard the story.

beside — besides. Beside means *next to*: **beside** the chair. **Besides** means *also, in addition, moreover,* etc.: She's not very pretty; **besides,** she has no money.

fiancé — fiancée. A man who is engaged to be married is someone's **fiancé** (one **e**); if it's a woman, she's a **fiancée** (two **e**'s). But both words are pronounced identically: fee-ahn-SAY.

effect — affect. An **effect** is an *idea* or *thing*: a scenic **effect**; what a stunning **effect** she produces; this will have a bad **effect** on production. **Affect,** on the other hand, is a verb meaning *to change, influence, move,* or *pretend*: this will **affect** production; she **affects** everyone strangely; his tears do not **affect** me; he **affected** a southern accent after he returned from Georgia. However — and be careful of this — if your verb has the special meaning of *bring about,* spell it **effect**: We shall try to **effect** (*bring about*) an improvement in production.

Check Your Learning

1. (Let, Leave) us go.
2. The thief was (hung, hanged).
3. These girls are all (alumnae, alumni) of the same college.
4. He was at first (incredible, incredulous) when he heard the news.
5. It's too expensive; (besides, beside) you don't really need it.
6. Her (fiancée, fiancé) is not very handsome, but he is rich.
7. How does this (affect, effect) you?
8. That is a strange and unpleasant (affect, effect).

Check your results: 1-Let; 2-hanged; 3-alumnae; 4-incredulous; 5-besides; 6-fiancé; 7-affect; 8-effect.

See How Much You've Improved

If you have worked conscientiously on Part V, you should be capable now of making a correct and confident choice in most or all of the sentences that follow. You can gauge your progress by the difference in your scores on the two major tests; but bear in mind that any error you make is a signal for careful review.

1. Between you and (I, me) I think he's completely dishonest.
2. Would you like to come with (he and I, him and me)?
3. I guess no one can handle this job except (her, she).

4. Was it (**she, her**) who called you?
5. We're not as well paid as (**them, they**).
6. You have accomplished more than (**me, I**) today.
7. Why don't you invite (**we, us**) and the Smiths?
8. (**Who, Whom**) do you wish to speak to?
9. (**Whom, Who**) did you say won first prize in the science fair?
10. Have they (**hung, hanged**) the murderer yet?
11. Your attitude (**effected, affected**) him strangely.
12. Do you think doctors will ever (**effect, affect**) a cure for cancer?
13. Aspirin has an almost immediate (**affect, effect**) on him.
14. That story is (**incredulous, incredible**).
15. I'd like to (**lay, lie**) down for a few minutes.
16. (**Lay, Lie**) your coat on the chair.
17. The wounded man (**laid, lied, lay**) on the street for over an hour before the ambulance arrived.
18. The papers have (**lain, laid**) on his desk all day.
19. When either of these calls (**comes, come**) in, let me know.
20. Neither of his parents (**is, are**) alive.
21. One of his first statements (**were, was**) completely wrong.
22. Congress or the President (**has, have**) to tackle this job.
23. The price of these books (**is, are**) considerably higher than last year.
24. (**Is, Are**) your sister and brother home from school yet?
25. (**Those, That**) memoranda (**are, is**) not what we want.

Check your results: 1-me; 2-him and me; 3-her; 4-she; 5-they; 6-I; 7-us; 8-Whom; 9-Who; 10-hanged; 11-affected; 12-effect; 13-effect; 14-incredible; 15-lie; 16-lay; 17-lay; 18-lain; 19-comes; 20-is; 21-was; 22-has; 23-is; 24-are; 25-those, are.

TWENTY-SIXTH DAY

Just for Fun

Those Pesky Pronouns

Pronouns are the most troublesome words in the English language. Actual tests have shown that these one-syllable tricksters pop up incorrectly in everyday speech more often than four- and five-syllable tongue twisters. **I** or **me**? **He** or **him**? **We** or **us**? **She** or **her**? **They** or **them**? **Who** or **whom**? Even experts stumble over these. Where do you stand? Try the following, checking the forms you think are right. Eleven or more correct answers makes your pronouns pets instead of pests:

1. Where can you find a better teacher than (**he, him**)?
2. No one except (**she, her**) can help you.
3. Let's keep this strictly between you and (**I, me**).
4. The baby looks more like (**I, me**) every day.
5. Everyone agreed to the change but (**we, us**).
6. Was it (**they, them**) the letter referred to?
7. Under these circumstances, how would you like to be (**we, us**)?
8. He wants you and (**I, me**) to come to the party.
9. Would you like to have dinner with my parents and (**I, me**)?
10. We are as good as (**they, them**) any day.
11. What would the girls do without (**we, us**) boys?
12. (**Who, Whom**) would you like to be if you were not yourself?
13. He is the only judge (**who, whom**) we think is capable of conducting that trial.
14. We will work with (**whoever, whomever**) has been assigned to teach the class.

Check your results: 1-he; 2-her; 3-me; 4-me; 5-us; 6-they; 7-we; 8-me; 9-me; 10-they; 11-us; 12-Who; 13-who; 14-whoever.

Proud of Your Past?

Can you write the correct past and perfect tenses of the following verbs? Sample: **write, wrote, has written.**

1. flee
2. fly
3. drink
4. swim
5. hang (a criminal)
6. lay
7. lie
8. lead
9. strive

Check your results: 1-fled, fled; 2-flew, flown; 3-drank, drunk; 4-swam (or swum), swum; 5-hanged, hanged; 6-laid, laid; 7-lay, lain; 8-led, led; 9-strove, striven.

What Do You Know About Babies?

A baby dog is a **puppy,** a baby cat is a **kitten.** Do you know what each of the following is called when it's a baby?

1. bear
2. cod
3. deer
4. duck
5. elephant
6. goose
7. hen
8. sheep
9. mare
10. horse

Check your results: 1-cub; 2-codling; 3-fawn; 4-duckling; 5-calf; 6-gosling; 7-chick, pullet; 8-lamb; 9-filly; 10-colt, foal.

What Do You Know About Plurals?

Almost all English words are pluralized by the simple process of adding **-s** or **-es**, but not the following ten. Can you give the correct plural for each word?

1. insigne _____
2. libretto _____
3. madame _____
4. locus _____
5. larva _____
6. datum _____
7. analysis _____
8. alumnus _____
9. alumna _____
10. criterion _____

Check your results: 1-insignia; 2-libretti; 3-mesdames; 4-loci; 5-larvae; 6-data; 7-analyses; 8-alumni; 9-alumnae; 10-criteria.

What Do You Know About Groups?

Animals, things, people are often found in distinctive groups. Can you give the name which properly describes a group of each of the following?

1. puppies _____
2. ants _____
3. actors _____
4. wolves _____
5. goats _____
6. fish _____
7. bees _____
8. chicks _____
9. worshipers _____
10. stars _____

Check your results: 1-litter; 2-colony; 3-troupe, company; 4-pack; 5-flock; 6-school, shoal; 7-colony, hive, swarm; 8-brood; 9-congregation; 10-constellation.

PART VI

The Final Days

In this closing part of the book, some additional aids are given to help you to a greater understanding of our English language.

TWENTY-SEVENTH DAY

How Would You Solve These Five Grammar Problems?

Like or as? Me or I? None are or none is? Between or among? Sure or surely? How do you usually say it, and are you right or wrong?

When you come right down to it, there's nothing we notice so quickly (nor, sometimes, with such ill-concealed delight) as the other fellow's mistakes. And, of course, there's nothing we're usually so blind to as our own errors.

This all-too-human reaction occurs just as regularly in respect to the use of words as it does in regard to dress, table manners, or morals.

But when it comes to English, we must bear in mind that any living language is a tricky business. Knowing formal principles is often only the first step, for while grammatical rules are stable enough, actual observance of them varies from time to time and from place to place. So there is a second step to take—namely, realizing that "correctness" is a highly relative and changeable term, that yesterday's error has a very good chance of being today's acceptable usage.

Here are some notes on modern trends in grammar that will keep you right up to the minute. They have been prepared by polling four selected groups of people who use the English language professionally — thirty-three editors, seven book reviewers, thirty-one well-known authors, and eleven professors of English in leading universities.

Test Yourself

Check up on your own speech by deciding whether the boldface words in the test sentences are perfectly *correct* (C) for everyday usage, or whether they are far enough removed from good English to be marked *doubtful* (D). Then compare your views with the opinions offered in the explanatory paragraphs that follow the test.

1. He's not doing his work **like** I told him to. _____
2. He acts more like **you and I** every day. _____
3. None of the houses **are** cheap enough. _____
4. She's having difficulty choosing **between** three dresses. _____
5. "Are you going to invite Bob and Dorothy?" — "**Sure!**" _____

Check your results:

1-D. What possible objection can there be to the word **like** as it appears in our test sentence? Notice the verb **told**; formal grammar claims that **like** is a preposition, and therefore may not be followed by a verb. In a construction like this one, says the rule, as or as if should be substituted, whichever conjunction fits.

Many educated speakers have a deep-seated aversion to **like** before a verb, and in the poll the vote was sixty-two against the test sentence, only twenty for. Ilka Chase, noted author and actress, made this typical comment on her questionnaire: "I realize that this use of the word **like** is commonplace, but to my way of thinking it is inexcusable, marking the speaker as grossly uneducated."

One must admit, nevertheless, that **like** with a verb is fairly prevalent, particularly in the southern and western states of the nation. Harry S Truman, a true Missourian in his speech patterns, described his reaction to the news of Franklin Roosevelt's sudden death in the following terms: "I felt like the moon, the stars, and all the planets had fallen on me."

And perhaps you have heard of the song that Eddie Cantor made so popular: "If you knew Suzie like I know Suzie," not to mention the recent commercial, "Winston tastes good, like a cigarette should."

Everything considered, and weighing all the pros and cons, I think we must conclude that **like** before a verb is still a controversial, though not necessarily uneducated, usage. To be 100 per cent safe, and to avoid any possibility of criticism, it is probably wise to stick to **as** or **as if** in formal speech and writing.

2-D. Here we are dealing with a usage which isn't a bit controversial. Since **like** is not followed by a verb, it is functioning in this sentence as a standard, honest-to-goodness preposition; as such, it is preferably used with **me**, an objective pronoun, rather than **I**, a nominative pronoun. Phrases like "between you and I," "like you and I," "except you and I," etc. (**between, like, except** are prepositions) are rarely, if ever, heard in educated speech. Correct form: "He acts more like you and **me** every day."

3.-C. In many newspapers, and in a good deal of formal writing, you will find **none** used with a *singular* verb. If you have noticed this phenomenon, and been puzzled by it, you will be relieved to learn that the usage is based on an antiquated principle of English grammar. This outmoded rule holds that since **none** originally meant **not one**, it must always be considered singular in form. Maybe it is singular in *form*, but it is sometimes so obviously plural in *meaning* that in all good sense we cannot, I submit, insist on using it only with a singular verb. This opinion is corroborated by the respondents to the poll, who accepted the test sentence by a vote of seventy-three to nine. When Sterling Andrus Leonard, until his recent death professor of English at Wisconsin University, made a survey of current English usage for the National Council of Teachers of English, he concluded that **none . . . are** is established English. Professor Leonard quoted one authority as saying: "It is pure priggishness to pretend that **none** is always singular."

It all boils down to this: in expressions like "none of the houses," "none of the girls," etc., the implication is strongly plural. Feel perfectly free, therefore, to use a plural verb.

4-C. **Between** for two things, **among** for three or more, is a rule honored by tradition but, more often than not, ignored in actual usage. The *American College Dictionary* says that in instances "in which each object is individually related to the rest, **between** is used of more than two . . .", and the *Merriam-Webster Collegiate Dictionary*, making the same point, offers as an example: "The three survivors had but one pair of shoes **between** them."

Weighing the merits of each dress against each of the others, the young lady is making a choice **between** the three dresses; to use **among** in this sentence would, I think, sound awkward and ridiculously stilted. In any similar situation, **between** is absolutely correct, even if more than two things are involved.

This sentence was accepted by the overwhelming ratio of seventy-one to eleven.

5-C. There was very little disagreement among the judges on this usage. The college professors and book reviewers accepted it unanimously, and only six authors and three editors cast negative notes. It is a common American tendency to shorten adverbs; Go **slow**, for example, is more popular than "go **slowly**." And **"Sure!"** as an enthusiastic answer to a question is at least as acceptable as **"Surely!"** though the latter may have a politer and somewhat more formal air. I think it is especially inadvisable and certainly unrealistic for parents to correct children who are in the habit of responding, "sure!" to a request. Youngsters are linguistically very imitative, and pick up expressions from their social environment; forcing a child to say **surely!** when he does not normally do so will make his speech conspicuous and perhaps tend to reduce his popularity among his friends. Considering the opinions of the professional people who responded to the poll, **surely** versus **sure** is far less important than some parents seem to think.

TWENTY-EIGHTH DAY

Seven New Problems to Pit Your Wits Against

> *Is a singular or plural verb used after **who**? What is the difference between **childlike** and **childish**? When do you feel **bad**, when **badly**? Which is correct, **we boys** or **us boys**? More excursions into the kind of pesky little problems that make English so difficult.*

If you have an idea that English is a difficult, subtle, and complicated language, full of pitfalls and booby traps for the unwary, you are 100 per cent right!

Even though grammar is today considerably more liberal than ever before, certain pesky problems continually arise in an active day's conversation. For instance: Which is correct, **data is** or **data are**? When do you **feel bad** and when do you **feel badly**? Is innocence **childish**, or is it **childlike**? Should you say **we girls** or **us girls**? and so on, without end.

Test Yourself

Pit your wits against some problems that are likely to confront you in your own everyday speech. Decide whether each of the following usages is *right* (R) or *wrong* (W). See how often you can come to a proper decision without rushing to the nearest dictionary or grammar text.

1. It is I who is responsible for his safety. ____
2. She is one of those girls who **flirts** with all the boys in the class. ____

3. Do you like **these** insignia? ____
4. Joan has a **childlike** innocence that is most refreshing. ____
5. I feel **badly** about your illness. ____
6. **Us** boys certainly stole a march on the girls that time! ____
7. You can't talk that way to **we** girls. ____

Check your results:

1-W. Here we have an extremely bookish, not to say downright erudite, way of expressing oneself. Most people would happily settle for "I am the one who is responsible for his safety," and thereby avoid a nasty grammatical pitfall; so if you insist on couching the thought in more scholarly language, you had better stick to strict grammar and say "It is I who **am** responsible for his safety." **Who** is a pronoun of changeable nature, taking whatever verb is required by its antecedent—that is, the word it refers to, which in this sentence is **I**. Since **I** is naturally followed by **am**, so also is **who** in the usage under discussion. The pattern is **I who am, you who are, he who is, one who is,** and so on right down the line.

2-W. **Who,** as we decided in problem 1, takes the verb required by its antecedent, which in this case is **girls.** Girls flirt; therefore, "She is one of those **girls** who **flirt** with all the boys in the class." Or you may wish to apply a test of logic. "She is one of those girls." Which girls? "Those girls who flirt with all the boys in the class." Grammatically or logically, **flirt** is the proper form.

3-R. **Insignia** is, technically speaking, a plural word, though probably not one person out of a hundred knows its singular form, **insigne,** pronounced in-SIG'-nee. (This piece of information will give you a decided advantage over your most intellectual friends.) To be superlatively correct, we should say either "**This insigne is** most impressive" or "**These insignia are** most impressive." But to be realistic, we must recognize that **insignia,** which neither looks nor sounds like a conventional plural noun, is being very widely used as a singular in cultivated speech.

4-R. The sense of this sentence is complimentary. The speaker is implying, by means of the adjective **refreshing,** that he finds the sophistication of most girls somewhat tiresome and is **glad** to have found one girl who still possesses the unsullied innocence of childhood. **Childlike** and **childish** are essentially the same in meaning; it is their emotional flavor that is different. **Childish** indicates a derogatory attitude: childish fear, childish stubbornness, childish temper. **Childlike,** on the other hand, is used to describe characteristics which are considered admirable: childlike innocence, childlike charm, childlike trust.

5-R. You may wonder what objection anyone can have to this sentence, but a quick inspection of some of the older grammar manuals will show that this use of **badly** was once darkly frowned upon. Why? Because the verb **feel,** according to strict rule, takes the adjective **bad,** not the adverb **badly.** Comparison is made with "It feels **soft**" (not **softly**) and "I feel **sick**" (not **sickly**).

However, strict rules do not always hold in educated speech, and to indicate mental distress many cultivated people habitually say "I feel **badly,**" perhaps because such phrasing has none of the implication of wickedness or mischievousness that might be understood from "I feel **bad.**" In a poll conducted recently, seven out of eleven college professors, twenty-six out of thirty-one authors, six out of seven book reviewers, and thirty-one out of thirty-three editors accepted the sentence under discussion as perfectly correct English.

6-W. Although no literate person in his right mind ever uses the pronoun **us** as subject of a verb, **us boys** in the same capacity may not sound too impossible to the unsophisticated ear. Hence the problem.

If you are ever in doubt about whether to say **we** or **us** in a situation like this, think of the sentence without the noun which follows the doubtful pronoun. By this means you will be able to resist any temptation to choose the incorrect form. Proper usage: "**We** certainly stole a march . . ."; therefore, "**We** boys certainly stole a march . . ."

7-W. The sentence without the noun **girls** will indicate the proper usage: "You can't talk that way to **us**"; therefore, "You can't talk that way to **us** girls."

TWENTY-NINTH DAY

Eight Final Problems and How to Tackle Them

When are we disinterested, when **uninterested**? *Is phenomenon singular or plural? How about measles, mathematics? Is it all right to use* **due to** *as a conjunction? Is* **try and come** *good English? Is* **older than me** *correct? Some more notes on present-day educated standards in American English.*

No doubt you have heard about the woman who stopped at the meat counter of a supermarket.

"A pound of kiddlies, please," she said.

The butcher stared at the customer in disbelief. Collecting his wits at last, he inquired hopefully, "Don't you mean *kidneys*, madam?"

The answer was immediate and very much annoyed: "Well, I *said* kiddlies, did'll I?"

The classic story about the New York urchin illustrates the same point. The boy was sitting in his third-grade classroom one sunny spring day when a sparrow lighted on the window sill.

"Teacher! Teacher!" he screamed in delight. "Look! A boid!"

"No, Johnnie," said the teacher, who for months had been wearily struggling to correct the children's English. "That's not a *boid*—it's a *bird*."

"Oh." The child was crestfallen, and more than a little puzzled. "It sure *looks* like a boid."

As you see, you can't always trust your own ears. Expressions which you use habitually may sound perfect to you, but what do your listeners think of them? On the other hand, certain usages that are quite common in educated circles, and therefore 100 per cent correct English, may offend you.

Test Yourself

Some of the sentences that follow are good English. Others would rarely, if ever, be heard in cultivated speech. Check up on your own language patterns by marking each underlined expression *right* (R) or *wrong* (W), then compare your reactions to the opinions given in the explanations.

1. I'm sorry, but I'm **disinterested** in your problems. _____
2. The reason she's fat is **because** she eats too much. _____
3. It's **a phenomena,** that's what it is! _____
4. Measles **is** catching. _____
5. Mathematics **are** a fascinating subject. _____
6. **Due to** a bad cold, he stayed home. _____
7. Please **try and** come early. _____
8. She's much older than **me.** _____

Check your results:

1-W. Do you think that **disinterested** is a more elegant and more erudite way of saying **uninterested?** Then you are laboring under a misconception.

If you're bored by discussions of early Roman civilization, you're **uninterested.** If you're indifferent to the blandishments of the canvasser at your door and would rather get back to your homework than listen to his sales talk, you're still **uninterested.**

Then when are you **disinterested?** Only when you are neutral, unbiased, or not personally involved in an issue. Two people who have a dispute often go to a third, **disinterested** party for an objective and impartial opinion. Judges are required by law to be **disinterested** in the cases tried before them. It would be most unfortunate for all concerned, however, if they were also **uninterested.**

In short, the two words have different meanings. Don't use one when you mean the other.

2-R. Those English teachers who are still bravely attempting to make their students say "The reason . . . is **that**" instead of the popular and perfectly logical "The reason . . . is **because**" are, I submit, waging a losing battle. The teachers base their argument on an involved grammatical abracadabra about copulative verbs taking noun, not adverbial, clauses; and the students (even the few who may understand what all this means) go out into the world armed with this precept only to find that adults whose wisdom and respectability are beyond question write and say "The reason . . . is **because**" more often than not. I leave it to you to imagine the confusion that results from this discrepancy between theory and practice.

Writing in a recent issue of *College English,* Professor Russel Thomas, a member of the Committee on Current English Usage of the National Council of Teachers of English, reports: "The evidence which I have gathered shows that 'The reason . . . is **because**' type of sentence has become established as good colloquial and literary English."

3-W. **Phenomena** is one of the many paradoxes in the English language. It looks and sounds like a singular word, but it is completely and definitely plural, and is so treated in good usage. We may say admiringly, "It's a **phenomenon,** that's what it is!" but we restrict the form **phenomena** to plural patterns, such as "Those **phenomena** are difficult to explain." **Criteria,** another paradox, has similar forms: **one criterion, many criteria.** However, **data** and **insignia** have crossed the line; though strictly plural, they are now widely used as singulars, probably because their true singular forms, **datum** and **insigne,** are so rarely heard.

4-R. You can't always judge by appearances: **phenomena** and **criteria** look singular, but are plural. **Measles** looks like a plural, but it's singular. Obviously you cannot have one **measle,** and since **measles** refer to a single disease, it is correctly used with **is**. Likewise **mumps, rickets, shingles,** and other such interesting diseases that end in -s.

5-W. **Mathematics,** though it perversely ends in **-s,** is singular; it is *one* science, just as **measles** is *one* disease. Therefore, mathematics **is** a fascinating subject. However, when the word is used as other than the name of a science, it is usually plural, as in "Let's figure the example again—I think your mathematics **are** wrong somewhere."

6-R. "This use of **due to**," says Margaret M. Bryant, Professor of English at Brooklyn College, "developed in the seventeenth century and has been constantly employed ever since, not only popularly, but also by magazine and editorial writers, as well as by authors of great distinction, among whom we may mention John Galsworthy."

If you have any friends of pedantic inclination, they will raise their eyebrows in shocked disapproval whenever you say **due to** where they would prefer **owing to** or **because of,** but I suggest you stand your ground. You have wide authority on your side.

7-R. Here is a perfect example of how our language sometimes blithely ignores the restrictions placed upon it by academic grammar. (The strict rule requires **to** in place of **and.**) Such giants of English literature as John Milton, Samuel Johnson, George Eliot, and Matthew Arnold frequently used **try and** in their writing. Isn't it then a bit stuffy to claim, as the purists do, that you and I are speaking bad English if we use it in our everyday conversation?

I wonder how these purists would react to the following bit of typical dialogue between two belligerent motorists: "I have a good mind to punch you right in the nose!" "Oh, yeah? Well, just **try and!**" Would they suggest that the second speaker, in the heat of argument, remember the rules of formal grammar and say "Well, just **try to**"?

8-W. "It's **me**" is good English—it has been sanctified by educated usage. "Older than **me,**" however, has received no such sanction. **I** is the preferred pronoun in this type of construction since the complete sentence is "She's much older than I **am**." Similarly, you're richer than **she** (is), I can drink more Scotch than **he** (can), they're smarter than **we** (are), and we eat more than **they** (do). If this is a little on the confusing side, you'll agree with the well-known humorist, Stephen Leacock, who said, "English pronouns are a disorderly and drunken lot. We no sooner straighten them up on one side than they fall over on the other."

THIRTIETH DAY

Just for Fun

Are You Quick with Words?

Words are dealt with at varying rates: an average reader can cover two hundred and fifty to three hundred a minute; a speaker can utter about two hundred a minute without rushing; a good typist cruises along at more than sixty a minute once she hits her stride; and without undue haste most people can write about twenty-five a minute in legible longhand.

But how fast can you *think* of words? Here is a short test of the speed of your verbal responses. You will find below forty simple words, and your problem is to think of, and write in the appropriate space, a synonym for each beginning with the letters **la**. (For example, the answer to 1 is **lather**.) The idea is to get through all forty as rapidly as possible.

This is not a test of your vocabulary, as every response required is a common word used in everyday conversation, but rather a measurement of the time you take to react to a verbal stimulus. Grab a pen or pencil, and either time yourself or have someone time you, using a timepiece with a second hand. Ready? *Go!*

1. foam   _____
2. put   _____
3. big   _____
4. final   _____
5. crippled   _____

6. work _____
7. legal _____
8. girl _____
9. pond _____
10. den _____
11. ticket _____
12. prank _____
13. spoon _____
14. lock _____
15. speech _____
16. maze _____
17. absence _____
18. lasso _____
19. regret _____
20. dull _____
21. cupboard _____
22. boy _____
23. loose _____
24. spear _____
25. path _____
26. nonprofessional _____
27. thickness _____
28. attorney _____
29. avalanche _____
30. thievery _____
31. slothful _____
32. enduring _____
33. principle _____
34. whip _____
35. funny _____
36. extravagant _____
37. wash _____
38. praise _____
39. descend _____
40. slim _____

Check your results: 1-lather; 2-lay (*or* laid); 3-large; 4-last; 5-lame; 6-labor; 7-lawful; 8-lass (*or* lassie); 9-lake (*or* lagoon); 10-lair; 11-label; 12-lark; 13-ladle; 14-latch; 15-language; 16-labyrinth; 17-lack; 18-lariat; 19-lament (*or* lamentation); 20-lackluster; 21-larder; 22-lad; 23-lax; 24-lance; 25-lane; 26-lay (*or* laic, laical); 27- layer; 28-lawyer; 29-landslide; 30-larceny; 31-lazy; 32-lasting; 33-law; 34-lash; 35-laughable; 36-lavish; 37-launder (*or* lave); 38-laud (*or* laudation); 39-land; 40-lank (*or* lanky).

Speed chart: four and a half to five minutes, slow; four to four and a half minutes, average; three and a half to four minutes, above average; two and a half to three and a half minutes, superior; under two and a half minutes, amazing.

Your score is valid if you have thirty-five or more correct answers.

They Don't Sound the Way They Look

Many English words are not pronounced the way they're spelled. For example, look at these:

quay (an artificial wharf): KEE
kiln (a large furnace for drying bricks): KILL
solder (a metal used to join other metals): SODDER
victuals (food): VITTLES
slough (a swamp): SLOO
phthisic (tuberculosis): TIZIK
Sioux (an Indian tribe): SOO
viscount (title of honor): VYECOUNT
colonel (army officer): KERNEL
fjord (inlet of the sea): FYORD
imbroglio (complicated situation): IM-BRŌL'-YO

Jog Your Vocabulary

Here are brief definitions of ten common English verbs that end in **-ate**. You probably know them all. But allowing yourself only two minutes, how many can you think of before time runs out?

1. to make easier _____ate
2. to tell _____ate
3. to chew _____ate
4. to speed up _____ate
5. to free _____ate
6. to make impure _____ate
7. to dig _____ate
8. to remove by surgery _____ate
9. to ruin _____ate
10. to make up for _____ate

Check your results: 1-facilitate; 2-relate; 3-masticate; 4-accelerate; 5-liberate; 6-adulterate; 7-excavate; 8-amputate; 9-devastate; 10-compensate.

Test Your Verbal Speed

Do you have a good strong, *responsive* vocabulary? Is it easy for you to pull words out of the deep recesses of your mind on a second's notice? Are you able to react with great speed upon exposure to certain verbal stimuli?

You can answer all these questions in ten minutes or less. In each of the tests to follow, read the instructions carefully, analyze the sample questions and answers so that you're sure you know what will be required of you, and then allow yourself exactly two minutes to complete each test.

Your verbal speed is excellent if you can write eight or more correct answers in each test before time is called.

Take as long as you wish to read the directions and analyze the samples; start timing only when you've actually begun the test. You get a hundred and twenty seconds on each complete group — that's an average of twelve seconds per item for recognizing the stimulus, reacting to it, and writing down your answer. It's no cinch—think you can do it?

Test 1

Write a word beginning with the letter k to satisfy each definition. Samples: an insect—**katydid**; Eskimo canoe—**kayak**.

1. German ruler   K_____
2. animal   k_____
3. sovereign   k_____
4. a rascal   k_____
5. a horseman   k_____
6. to weave   k_____
7. Mohammedan Bible   K_____
8. wisdom   k_____
9. doghouse   k_____
10. color   k_____

Check your results: 1-Kaiser; 2-kangaroo, koala; 3-king; 4-knave; 5-knight; 6-knit, knot; 7-Koran; 8-knowledge; 9-kennel; 10-khaki.

Test 2

Write a word that fits each definition and that ends in the letters -ential. The initial letter is supplied to speed your reaction. Samples: pertaining to the highest elective office in this country—**presidential**; fortunate—**providential**.

1. private, secret   c_____ential
2. showing regard for another's wishes, respectful   d_____ential
3. necessary   e_____ential
4. of no great importance, trivial   i_____ential
5. possessing power or effect   i_____ential

146

6. pertaining to contagious disease
   or plagues   p_____ential
7. possible, though not yet actual   p_____ential
8. showing favor   p_____ential
9. connected with living abodes   r_____ential
10. rushing, overwhelming (like a
    rapid stream)   t_____ential

Check your results: 1-confidential; 2-deferential; 3-essential; 4-inconsequential; 5-influential; 6-pestilential; 7-potential; 8-preferential; 9-residential; 10-torrential.

Test 3

Write a word having the same meaning as each key word, and starting with the letters **va**. Samples: a variety show—**vaudeville**; residence of the Pope—**Vatican**.

1. empty   va_____
2. wanderer   va_____
3. conceited   va_____
4. manservant   va_____
5. courage   va_____
6. disappear   va_____
7. conquer   va_____
8. change   va_____
9. a safe   va_____
10. worthwhile   va_____

Check your results: 1-vacant, vapid, vacuous, vacuum; 2-vagabond, vagrant; 3-vain; 4-valet; 5-valor; 6-vanish; 7-vanquish; 8-vary, variety; 9-vault; 10-valuable.

Test 4

Write a word opposite in meaning to the key word and starting with letter **W**. Samples: outside—**within**; summer—**winter**.

1. sleep   w_____
2. peace   w_____
3. cold   w_____
4. careless   w_____
5. conserve   w_____
6. strong   w_____
7. poverty   w_____
8. ill   w_____
9. part, portion   w_____
10. foolishness   w_____

Check your results: 1-wake; 2-war; 3-warm; 4-wary, watchful, watching, wily; 5-waste; 6-weak; 7-wealth; 8-well; 9-whole; 10-wisdom, wit.

Test 5

Each of the following nouns has an adjective form, entirely different from it in appearance and sound. Write the adjective which starts with the given letter. Samples: hand—**manual**; moon—**lunar**.

1. year   a_____
2. body   a_____
3. king   r_____
4. barber   t_____
5. tooth   d_____

148

6. foot   p_____
7. tree   a_____
8. doctor   m_____
9. mouth   o_____
10. church   e_____

Check your results: 1-annual; 2-anatomical; 3-royal, regal; 4-tonsorial; 5-dental; 6-pedal, podiatric, podial; 7-arboreal; 8-medical; 9-oral; 10-ecclesiastic, ecclesiastical.